Wine Wisdom

A Collection of Quotes, Toasts, Mirth and Merriment

May you enjoy the wit and wisdom of the "women" I have assembled for this book.

[signature]

Wine Wisdom

A Collection of Quotes, Toasts, Mirth and Merriment

By George A. LaMarca
Illustrations by J.P. Schmelzer

First Edition

2004

VANTAGE PRESS
NEW YORK

FIRST EDITION

Published by Vantage Press, Inc.
419 Park Avenue South, New York, New York, 10016

ISBN 0 533 14919 3 . . . . .Printed in U.S.A.

Library of Congress Catalog Card Number 2004092691

Dedicated
to
my wife Angela.

ABOUT THE AUTHOR

Using his research and investigative skills as a trial lawyer, George A. LaMarca has uncovered and compiled hundreds of toasts, salutations, and words of wisdom on the role that wine has played throughout the ages in social rituals, health, love, friendship, religion, and the celebration of life.

Mr. LaMarca is a senior shareholder in the Des Moines, Iowa law firm of LaMarca & Landry, P.C. He graduated from Drake University School of Law in 1970 and is licensed to practice in Iowa and Florida and before the United States Supreme Court.

As a Past President of the Iowa Trial Lawyers Association, he served as a member of its Executive

Committee for five years and as a member of its Board of Governors for ten years. In 1989 the Iowa Trial Lawyers Association named him Member of the Year. Mr. LaMarca is certified as a Civil Trial Advocate by the National Board of Trial Advocacy. Mr. LaMarca is a Diplomat of the American Board of Professional Liability Attorneys. His extensive litigation experience is demonstrated by his rank of Advocate from the American Board of Trial Advocacy.

George is a frequent lecturer at state and nationwide seminars for lawyers, paralegals and legal investigators. He has authored numerous articles on litigation practice issues and topics which have been published in a variety of respected legal treatises and journals. He has served on the editorial boards of a number of professional journals in the fields of both law and medicine and he is currently a member of the Board of Editors of the Trial Diplomacy Journal.

Other than some short magazine pieces on fishing and travel, this is Mr. LaMarca's first non-legal work.

ABOUT THE ILLUSTRATOR

John Schmelzer has been drawing since long before he had his first glass of wine. It's a shame it took so long to marry the pleasures.

Mr. Schmelzer's work has appeared in many publications over his long career, The Chicago Tribune, Esquire Magazine, Playboy, ABA Journal, and Voir Dire Magazine are just a few. He has also done work for children's publications, for advertising agencies, and for many companies around the United States. His illustration has appeared in the Society of Illustrators Annual and Graphis Magazine, and his work has won awards in advertising competitions in New York, Chicago, Milwaukee, and Madison, Wisconsin.

Wine Wisdom

A Collection of Quotes, Toasts, Mirth and Merriment

Contents

xi

"*The wisdom of the wise and the experience of ages, may be preserved by quotations.*"
Isaac D'Israeli

Preface

The object of this compilation is a thought provoking ride through the universe of wine consumption – by camelback, not a rocket. The breadth of this journey is incredible. An apt summary of wine's immense role in all aspects of nearly all societies was set forth by Martin Elkort in his book, *The Secret Life of Food*: "Pull the cork from a bottle of wine and you let a genie out that has given pleasure to much of the world since humans first tasted grapes. The story of wine encompasses most of history, and is drawn from every corner of the world and every economic level of society. It embraces agriculture, science, history, commerce, art, literature, and legend." In contrast, most dictionary definitions pale and do not even hint at the important role that wine has and continues to play in religion, health, and celebrations. An example follows:

> **wine** (win), *n.* [L. *vinum*], 1. the fermented juice of grapes, used as an alcoholic beverage, and in cooking, etc. 2. the fermented juice of other fruits or plants: as, dandelion wine.
> *Webster's New World Dictionary of the American Language*, 1968

There is actually a standard definition of wine, drawn up by the Wine & Spirit Association: "Wine is the alcoholic beverage obtained from the fermentation of freshly gathered grapes, the fermentation of which has been carried through in the district of origin, according to local traditions and practice." While accurate and informative, the shortfalls of this definition have been squarely and deservedly framed by John Baldwinson in his book *Plonk and Superplonk*. His attack is as follows: "It says nothing about the pleasures of wine: the complexities of colours, tastes, smells, associations. It says nothing about the glow that a good wine can give you, or about its being a natural (some say, living) product. It says nothing about it being good for you; above all, I wish it said something about the way wine makes you happy."

Thus, the object of this work will take us to sources of wine wisdom beyond the dictionary and industry definitions into a wide variety of literary sources from the biblical to the bawdy and nearly everything in between.

Acknowledgements

Inherent in this book is the recognition that the sources for quotes, toasts, sayings, and poems in this work are the ideas and work product of hundreds of people, dead and alive, and where the author was known, I have given them credit. A number of passages are not cited as to author or source, and that is because I was unable to determine the originator of the work or it was found in another work also uncited as to source.

A special thanks to Connie Wabeke of Johnston, Iowa, who assisted in my research and who also typed and helped edit the many drafts of this work; and also to Attilio Negro, M.D., of Greensberg, Pennsylvania, who provided valuable overall critique and assisted with format editing of the Glossary. The author also wishes to acknowledge the biographical research of Chad Knapp, Mark Hudson, and Nick Bailey on the persons who have been quoted in this book and listed in the Glossary, and the final proofing by LuAnn Hood, Sara Lamme, and Brooke Wenck. The illustrator would like to thank Melanie Hallam for her technical assistance in the translation of the graphic design of this book into language that a computer could understand.

Introduction

The quoted passages herein demonstrate the significant role that wine has played in all aspects of human endeavors since nearly the beginning of the recording of time. No other potable liquid is more illustrative of what nature, aided by human industry, can achieve. Becoming more acquainted with what others have said, both wise and wily, will increase our understanding and reverence, as well as our enjoyment, of this immortal beverage.

Hopefully these passages will give us more delight of the wine in our glass as we gain more insight into wine in the lives of others throughout history. Indeed, winemaking was an integral part of the earliest agricultural societies, and its present day level of consumption and interest as a financial venture illustrates its enduring significance to our basic institutions.

While petrified grape seeds have been discovered in ancient cave dwellings, history begins to record winemaking in Italy since before the dawn of Western civilization. In the 5th Century B.C., Greek historian Thucydides chronicled that "the peoples of the Mediterranean began to emerge from barbarism when they learnt to cultivate the olive and the vine." The Romans were responsible for spreading the science of viniculture throughout Europe as they conquered new lands. The role of wine in Italy was not lost on the ancient Greeks who acknowledged the prominence wine played in Italy by calling the country Oenotria, "the land of trained vines." To this day, ancient Italian varieties such as Nebbiolo, Sangiovese, and Pino Grigio are major contributors to world wine production, both as pure wine from these grapes, or the blending backbone of many other styles of wine. These varieties are staples not only in Italy, but also in other parts of the world, particularly northern California.

The era 4000-3000 B.C. saw the fertile valleys extending from the Nile to the Persian Gulf cultivated with grape vines. The Phoenicians, Greeks, and Romans cultivated and distributed grapevines and winemaking knowledge. The Greeks attributed great wonders – physical and supernatural – to their gods. Dionysus (thirteenth god of the Greeks, a son of Zeus) is claimed in Greek mythology to have invented wine on Mount Nysa and was known as the "god of wine." An example of the pervasiveness of wine in Roman times is the number of Latin words to describe different states of consumption:

Ebriolus
Slightly tipsy

Ebriulatus
Tipsy

Ebriacus
Intoxicated

Uvidus
In one's cups

Vinolentus
Full of wine

Madescere
Drunk

Temulentus
Riotous drunk

Vino mersus
Dead drunk

A person who was in the habit of getting intoxicated on wine was *ebriositas*, an alcoholic. When such a person awoke from a drunken slumber, he was *sobrius*, which conveyed a temporary condition.

The Latin poet, Ausonius, around 380 A.D., mentions his fine vineyards in Bordeaux. Bordeaux's modern day pre-eminence began as a result of the marriage of French queen, Eleanor of Aquitanie to Henry II. When the English king married her in 1152, he acquired an enormous part of France in the bargain, and soon after gave great financial benefits to the Gascon wine merchants; thus contributing to the increased popularity of

Bordeaux in England where it is often referred to as Claret.

The Bible has hundreds of references to wine. Its passages embrace, extoll, and encourage wine-making and consumption in innumerable personal and social circumstances, with surprisingly little caution on overindulgence. The Old Testament contains numerous references giving insight into the importance of wine in early Hebrew culture. Noah is reported to have had a vineyard as one of his first endeavors after the flood. From the New Testament we know that bread and wine are the basic elements of Christian Eucharistic services.

From Roman foundations, great rulers such as Charlamagne in Europe and Queen Elizabeth I in Great Britain lent their power and encouragement to wine producing such that by the time of the American Revolution in 1776, Thomas Jefferson was encouraging the planting of European wine grapes in the new world. So proud was Jefferson of his vinicultural endeavors he opined: "By making this wine known to the public, I have rendered my country as great a service as if I had enabled it to pay back the national debt." Adding to Thomas Jefferson's endeavors to bring the wines of the old world to the new world, German settlers along the Rapidan River in Virginia planted large amounts of European grapes starting in 1710. Disease overtook the vines, however, and all of these vineyards eventually failed. In 1852, Charles Lefaranc, a Burgundian, settled in the Santa Clara Valley of California, and with cuttings from his native France established the first successful commercial vineyard in northern California. He became the founder of what was later called the Almaden Vineyards.

The multi-sensual and multi-dimensional nature of wine was only partially captured by this litany from King Edward VII: "One not only drinks wine, one smells it, tastes it, sips it, and one talks about it."

Wine played a significant role in financing the teaching of young men to become Jesuit priests in California. In 1888, the Jesuit fathers and brothers were having difficulty supporting the novice's training and also obtaining sacramental wine for serving Mass. Brother Louis Oliver sent a request home to Montpelier, France for cuttings of its best varietal grapes. The vineyard these Jesuit fathers started in 1888 is now known as the Novitiate Winery in Los Gatos at the foot hills of the Santa Cruz Mountains.

Many Italian-American immigrants, in the decades spanning 1850 to 1910, played a large role in the development and present day prominence of the California wine industry. These families imported Italian style wine such as Sangiovese, Barbera, Nebbiolo, Pino Grigo, and Pino Bianco. Not as influential with legislation as was Jefferson, these first generation Italian Americans hit a brick wall called Prohibition in 1919. The politicians responsible for Prohibition obviously did not understand their Jeffersonian history, and certainly did not understand the social and physical forces involved in mankind's consumption of alcohol. However, by the time our elected officials came to their senses and The Prohibition Act was repealed in 1933, only a few of these Italian-American families were able to rekindle their wine-making into a business. Their present day, legendary status in the American wine industry was marked by stalwart contributions. A notable list of these survivors include the families Bargetto, Gallo, Foppiano, Martini, Mondavi, Nervo, Parducci, Pedroncelli, Sebastiani, Seghesio and Simi.

Wine is part of the defining identity of France. This identity seems in many ways to be embraced in the very soul of being French. A fascinating account of this French affinity with wine can be

found in *Wine and War*, by Don and Petie Kladstrup.
The book gives vivid accounts of how, during two
world wars, the French risked their lives to save
vintage wine stocks, a cause that was not only
meant to protect their economy, but also save the
heart and soul of France. The Kladstrups attribute
the French love of the grape and devotion to wine
as part of their way of life as instrumental in
helping them survive and triumph over one of the
darkest and most difficult chapters in French
history. History also records other significant
contributions wine has made in a war. In the Sixth
Century, B.C., Cyrus the Great of Persia ordered his
troops to drink wine as an anecdote to infection
and illness. Julius Caesar considered wine a
provision as important as food for his elite troops.
Napoleon Bonaparte tried to bolster the morale
and the health of his troops by providing them
with wine whenever he could. In the footsteps of
Napoleon, Edouard Barther, a French government
deputy, called for establishing wine canteens at
allied military encampments during World War II.

Wine's role in the world today is no less
pervasive than its historical roles, and thus our
need to know as much as we can about it, abounds
as well. At last year's International Wine Challenge,
6,500 wines from 30 countries were tasted. More

7

than 200 wine festivals and charity auctions will be staged in the United States this year alone. Charity wine auctions have become a significant event and a substantial source of pooling money for highly worthy causes. *Wine Spectator* reports that in the United States, 186 charitable wine auctions were held in 1999. In 2000, charity wine auctions in the United States raised over $12 million with beneficiaries ranging from AIDS hospices to symphony orchestras. According to the Wine Institute, total wine sales in the U.S. for 2000 reached 565 million gallons, which is a three percent increase from 1999.

The year 1976 is considered a milestone for American wines. This is the year that British wine connoisseur and merchant Steve Spurrier made an investigation of northern California wines and became convinced that their quality was comparable to the best Europe had to offer. To see if he was not just swept up by the moment, he organized an elaborate and highly publicized blind tasting in Paris which matched two California wines, a 1973 Stags Leap (Cabernet Sauvignon) and 1973 Chateau Montelina (Chardonnay) which scored highest when matched against several top varieties of French Bordeaux (made from the Cabernet Sauvignon grape) and white burgundies

8

(Chardonnay grape). The Paris tasting, in addition to opening up new markets abroad for American wines, peaked European, Australian and African wine producers' interest in American methods of grape growing and wine production.

The French wine industry did not take the Paris results all that well and spirited debate continues to this day concerning this event. All things considered, the controversy may be "sour grapes" because the judges were top French wine connoisseurs. At least as to wine appreciation, we have become a global village. Because their clients' tastes demand it, many American restaurants offer fantastic selections of not only California wines, but also wines from all over the world. For example Martini House in St. Helena, California has an award winning wine list which, while in the middle of the Napa Valley, contains the following passage. "Why include wines from around the world? The Napa Valley wine industry is part of the global wine market and must compete with the best wines from France, Italy and Australia, etc. We offer selections from the world's finest appellations to provide the opportunity for comparisons with our Napa wines.
Now you can be the judge."

The University of California at Davis was an
innovator in what has now become a world class
program on viniculture and winemaking. Many of
the new vintners of the last two decades have
trained there, including not only those from the
United States, but also Europe, Australia and
South America. Beginning in the 1960s, better
marketing and better winemaking techniques aided
Americans in observing a difference between jug
wines and varietals. As a result, there was market
encouragement to cultivate varietals using old
world methods supplanted only with purposeful
modern techniques. Examples of winemaking
innovation which were truly progress and not
mere change were grape presses that are
computerized to calibrate the exact amount of
pressure required to extract maximum flavor and
minimum astringency from a particular varietal.
The speed of fermentation has been governed by
the development of heating and cooling jackets
surrounding stainless steel fermentation tanks.
These are perhaps the best examples of a
commitment to old world quality with
modern technique.

In the United States, "wine country" is no
longer an axiomatic synonym for Napa and Sonoma
Counties in California. At least ten other California

counties have substantial wine production.
While nearly 90 percent of U.S. wine is made in
California, other states are rapidly chopping away
at this statistic. Iowa, for example, has nearly
200 vineyards totaling a little over 400 acres with
approximately 20 wineries and a number in the
planning stages. The Somerset Inn and Winery in
Indianola, Iowa offers ten varieties of wine. They
have begun to promote winemaking along with
other significant agricultural crops. All 50 states
have at least one registered winery, with California
and Washington being the leaders. The States of
Indiana, Iowa, Kansas, Maryland, Missouri, New
York, Ohio, Oregon, Pennsylvania, Texas, Virginia,
Washington and West Virginia all have significant
wine producing acreages. In case you think the
wines from these other states do not compete with
northern California wines, the Tabor Winery of
Baldwin, Iowa received the "Best in Class" award
for its Iowa grown and produced Marechal Foch
Nouveau at the International Wine Competition
in Claremont, California in February, 2001.

Proving that everything new is old, Italy has
undergone a resurgence of its wine prominence in
the last twenty years after many decades of overall
decline and minimal bright spots. As a result, many

varieties of Italian wines now fetch the same price as the highest rated French Bordeauxs. Italy's resurgence has been crowned by the appearance of the 1997 vintage thought to be one of the greatest in the last fifty years. Leading the Italian vinicultural renaissance is popular winemaker Angelo Gaja, whose Barolo and Barbaresco wines in some cases command first-growth Bordeaux prices. Another highly visible midwife of Italy's rebirth is Piero Antinori, whose namesake winery is one of Tuscany's biggest and best wine producers. The Tuscan district of Brunello di Montelcino also produces memorable wines, many of which require at least a decade's aging before reaching their full and even longer lasting potential.

The American Center for Food, Wine and the Arts opened in 2001 in Napa, California (www.theamericancenter.com). Over $70 million was raised so that visitors can learn about food and wine on par with each other. Artistic performances and art exhibits will be woven into this tapestry of the good life. To get the center underway, visionary winemaker Robert Mondavi donated $20 million.

Betting on a never-ending fascination with both the process and the end product of wine-making, two famous California names,

Disney and Robert Mondavi, have collaborated to create a theme park adjacent to Disney Land in Anaheim, California called "Golden Vine Winery." The park is dedicated to educating Americans about the process of wine-making and the pleasures of wine drinking by taking you along pathways that cover all aspects of the activities in the vineyard and the winery with knowledgeable "wine ambassadors" to answer questions and guide visitors along the way. Included are tastings, lectures offering insight into the character of various wines, tips on serving wine, and wine and food pairings. In addition to film presentations, children receive a 16-page activity book explaining farming techniques and other aspects of planting and harvesting grapes. Aspiring chefs are offered assistance in the preparation of their own pasta dishes from prominent chefs. As championed by Robert Mondavi for years and in keeping with all other things Disney, the theme park embraces wine-making and its consumption with food as an integral part of an enjoyable and wholesome lifestyle.

It is unexplainable, but people who really love wine enjoy not only drinking it, but looking at it. Just as book lovers can browse for hours in libraries and bookstores, so do wine lovers browse for hours in well stocked wine stores. While the phrase "so many labels so little time" has not become commonplace, it is a common lament of wine lovers who browse through wine shops and wine catalogs. Unlike any other beverage, people not only drink wine, they also collect it. Great vintages from great vineyards are treated like an object d'art. They buy and collect wines from great vintages without ever intending to consume them. The values of the "greats" generally increase with age, but there are many risks – from spoilage to drinking. A combination of knowledge and luck can give collectors profits as well as pleasure from their cellars. Consider these auction highlights as reported in the September 15, 2000, issue of *Wine Spectator*.

Price	Wine	Quantity	Auction House	Date
$114,614	Château Mouton-Rothschild 1945	1 jeroboam	Christie's (London)	Sept. 1997
$112,500	Colgin 1992-1995	4 18-liter bottles	Zachys-Christie's (NY)	Dec. 1998
$109,324	Château Cheval-Blanc 1947	1 imperial	Christie's (London)	Sept. 1997
$91,691	Château Pétrus 1961	12 bottles	Christie's (London)	Sept. 1997
$88,165	Château Latour à Pomerol 1961	12 bottles	Christie's (London)	Sept. 1997
$63,000	Château La Mission-Haut-Brion 1949	1 jeroboam	Sherry-Lehmann with Sotheby's (New York)	Nov. 1999
$51,750	Château d'Yquem 1921	12 bottles	Sherry-Lehmann with Sotheby's (New York)	Nov. 1999
$46,000	DRC Romanée-Conti 1990	1 methuselah	Zachys-Christie's (NY)	Dec. 1997
$41,400	Paul Jaboulet Aîné Hermitage La Chapelle 1961	12 bottles	Sherry-Lehmann with Sotheby's (New York)	Nov. 1999
$36,687	Château Lafite Rothschild 1811	1 "tappit-hen" (magnum)	Christie's (London)	June 2000
$35,650	Château Lafleur 1959	5 magnums	Zachys-Christie's (NY)	Feb. 2000
$34,500	Château Latour 1945	12 bottles	Sherry-Lehmann with Sotheby's (New York)	Nov. 1999
$24,150	Château Pétrus 1982	12 bottles	Sotheby's (London)	March 2000
$24,150	Beaulieu Vineyard Cabernet Sauvignon Georges de Latour Private Reserve 1951	12 bottles	Zachys-Christie's (LA)	April 2000
$23,100	Dominus Estate 1991	1 imperial	Davis & Co. (Chicago)	Oct. 1997
$22,923	Château Palmer 1961	12 bottles	Christie's (London)	Feb. 2000
$21,850	Araujo Cabernet Sauvignon (1991-95)	5 double magnums	Zachys-Christie's (NY)	Nov. 1999
$18,975	Château Calon-Ségur 1947	12 bottles	Zachys-Christie's (LA)	April 2000
$17,250	Inglenook Cabernet Sauvignon 1941	3 bottles	Sherry-Lehmann with Sotheby's (New York)	Nov. 1999
$16,100	Colgin 1994	12 bottles	Zachys-Christie's (NY)	June 1998
$11,500	Screaming Eagle 1994	3 bottles	Zachys-Christie's (LA)	April 2000
$10,350	Bryant Family 1994	12 bottles	Zachys-Christie's (LA)	June 1998
$9,775	Dalla Valle Maya 1994	1 imperial	Zachys-Christie's (LA)	Nov. 1999
$8,050	Harlan Estate (1990-1995)	6 magnums	Zachys-Christie's (LA)	June 1998

When it comes to the value of a bottle of wine, product and price are not always a great pairing. Price does not guarantee quality and is more often a mere reflection of what the market will accept. Unlike most other products, production costs of wine have little to do with high prices. Many California reds that will not last five years (by design) are priced over $100 a bottle, yet some that will last more than ten years can be purchased for under $20. Fortunately, values are still abundantly available. David Coffaro, a Sonoma wine-maker, has made a crusade out of producing great reds that will last more than five years and for under $20 a bottle. He is the Ralph Nader of overrated and overpriced wines. His informative wine consumer pulpit is a weekly diary on his very entertaining web site, (www.coffaro.com).

Wine can also be bought as a commodity on a futures basis. Companies like Rare, L.L.C. (sales@rarefinewines.com) and The Wine Club (thewineclub.com) buy pre-release lots directly from the chateaux cellars in France and resell direct to you. A published rating system from barrel tasting is used to determine price.

Last, but not least, are the health benefits of wine. While some previous research assumed that it is alcohol which is the protective element, several recent comprehensive studies have concluded that it is the antioxidants and flavonoids in wine. White wines are as rich in antioxidants as certain fruits and vegetables, and red wines are much richer in antioxidants than all of them. The tannins, which give red wines their body and longevity, contain the antioxidants which not only have been found to inhibit heart problems and cancers, but also have been found to be antihistaminic and antiviral and slow the destruction of collagen in our tissues and skin. The unique health benefits of red wine are detailed in Section V, Wine and Health.

This book will offer both practical and entertaining information on wine. If you are looking for the perfect wine toast, you will find it in these pages. If you are looking for a reason to begin drinking wine, you will find it in these pages. If you are looking for a reason to drink more wine, you will find it in these pages. If you are looking for a reason to become more acquainted with the esoteric essence of wine, you will find it in these pages.

Chapter I

Wine and Celebration

Wine adds a festive note to any occasion from the simplest lunch at a park to a sumptuous meal at a fine restaurant. Raising a glass of wine or champagne has put the spark in many a gathering. Indeed, champagne and celebration are synonymous. With a glass of wine in hand at a gathering of two or more people, greetings, toasts, praise and words of wisdom are inevitable. The words of wisdom in this section not only cover the ages, but are ageless in their revelry of wine as the catalyst of celebration.

A waltz and a glass of wine invite an encore.
Johann Strauss

Wine is the flower in the buttonhole
of civilization.
Werumeus Buning

Is not wine the very essence of laughter?
Maurice des Ombiaux,
Le Gotha des vins de France, 1925

The object of dinner is not to eat and drink, but
to join in merrymaking and make lots of noise.
For that reason, he who drinks half drinks best.
Lin Yutang

The art in using wine is to produce the greatest possible quantity of present gladness, without any future depression. To this end, a certain degree of simplicity is essential, with due attention to seasons and kinds of food, and particularly to the rate of filling the glass. Too many sorts of wine confuse the palate and derange digestion.
Thomas Walker, *The Art of Dining*, 1881

There is no gladness without wine.
Babylonian Talmud, Pesachim

Work like you don't need money, love like you've never been hurt, and dance like no one is watching. Enjoy a glass of wine each day.
Anonymous

Everything in moderation – with a few glorious exceptions.
Robert Mondavi

It is well to remember that there are five reasons for drinking: the arrival of a friend, one's present or future thirst; the excellence of the wine; or any other reason.
Anonymous

Not all drinking is everyday drinking.
In everyone's life there are special occasions that
call for a celebration of one kind or another. We
drink to celebrate a marriage, an anniversary
or a birthday. We drink to celebrate the arrival
of a child, and to celebrate a promotion to a
new position. And sometimes we drink even in
sorrow, when someone we love has died. On
New Year's Eve we drink a toast to the year that
is being born — but we think of the year that is
dying, too. In fact, there is hardly any milestone
in life that doesn't slip past more gracefully and
memorably if we raise a glass to it. . . .
To drink is fine; to overdrink is pointless.
  Toots Shor

No holiday is complete without food and
wine. They just go together. Sort of like
friends and family.
  Emeril Lagasse

The Irish believe that fairies are extremely fond
of good wine. The proof of the assertion is that
in the olden days royalty would leave a keg of
wine out for them at night. Sure enough,
it was always gone in the morning.
  Irish Folklore

God in His goodness sent the grapes, to cheer
both great and small; little fools will drink
too much, and great fools not at all.
Anonymous

What better adapted than the festive use of
wine in the first place to test and in the second
place to train the character of a man, if care
be taken in the use of it? Where is there cheaper
or more innocent?
Plato

Drinks were served in golden goblets, goblets of
different kinds, and the royal wine was lavished
according to the bounty of the king. And
drinking was according to the law, no one was
compelled; for the king had given orders to all
the officials of his palace to do as every man
desired.
The Bible, Esther 1:7-8

But November 11 in France is not only
St. Martins Day — the patron saint of reformed
drunkards — but the feast of Bacchus, and the
event was celebrated centuries back by joyful
tasting of the new wine, or as Rabelais called it
"September Purée." It would come as no surprise
to read in Pantagruel, "Busvons, car Beausjolai
Nousveau est arrivé."
Jennifer Taylor

24

A toast:
May we always be as bubbly as this champagne!

I come to my garden, my sister, my bride,
I gather my myrrh with my spice, I eat my
honeycomb with my honey, I drink my wine
with my milk. Eat, O friends, and drink:
drink deeply, O lovers!
    The Bible, Song of Solomon 5:1

But the vine said to them, "Shall I leave my wine
which cheers gods and men, and go to sway
over the trees?"
    The Bible, Judges 9:13

Sparkling and bright in liquid light
Does the wine our goblets gleam in;
With hue as red as the rosy bed
Which a bee would choose to dream in.
Then fill to-night, with hearts as light
To loves as gay and fleeting
As bubbles that swim on the beaker's brim
And break on the lips while meeting.
    Charles Fenno Hoffman, "Sparkling and Bright"

He who clinks his cup with mine, adds a glory
to the wine.
    George Sterling

Wine is a part of society because it provides a
basis not only for a morality but also for an
environment; it is an ornament in the slightest
ceremonials of French daily life, from the
snack... to the feast, from the conversation at
the local café to the speech at a formal dinner.
Roland Barthes, *Mythologies, Wine and Milk*

For wine has participated universally in the
cultural ascent of man, serving as a festive
drink at his birth, a solemn drink at his death,
a sacred drink in religious ceremonies, and a
stimulant of discussion in symposium and
intellectual colloquia.
Dr. Salvatore P. Lucia

Chapter II
Wine and Food

The preparation of food is probably humanity's first skill or art. Cookbooks are said to be among the most widely published and read books of all time. It is not surprising then that a lot has been written about eating food with wine, and precisely what wines to enjoy with particular foods. What follows in this section are passages which discuss the benefits of consuming food and wine together. Having wine with food always makes a meal seem more like an occasion than a necessity. Perhaps the very presence of the wine reminds us that we should take our time to enjoy the food and savor each bite. With wine after a morsel, our palate is refreshed and our appetite made more eager with each successive sip.

Wine is not only enjoyed with food, but has become an essential ingredient of many classic dishes. According to Shirley Corriher, an acclaimed food scientist, alcohol is a flavor enhancer and heightens the flavors of all other ingredients in a recipe. *The Oxford Companion to Wine* tells us that the recipes of Apicius, the heralded Roman chef, show that wine was commonly used in his sauces and it has found a place in the kitchen ever since. In 1981, Julia Child, Dick Graf, and Robert Mondavi formed the American Institute of Wine and Food, with a goal of letting people know that drinking wine with food is good for them.

Many authors have given serious study (and presumably research) to pairing food with wine. This symbiotic endeavor has embraced pairing not only the classiest noveau French cuisine with wine, but also hamburgers and wine. *The Everything Wine Book* by Danny May and Andy Sharpe states "It is doubtful that any dining ritual has caused more needless anxiety than that of choosing the 'correct wine for dinner.' What a shame! We are talking about two very enjoyable foods — good food and good wine." After advising us that traditional wine and food matching rules were made to (and should) be broken on occasion, May and Sharpe recommend the following wine and food matches:

Chili – Beaujolais; Zinfandel
Grilled Steak – Cabernet Sauvignon;
    Shiraz/Syrah
Hamburger – Any inexpensive red wine
Roast Beef – Pinot Noir and Merlot
Steak Au Poivre – Big reds – Zinfandels from
    California and Rhones from France
Chicken (roasted) – almost any wine you like
Chicken (highly seasoned) – Chenin Blanc
    and Reisling
Duck/Goose/Game Birds – Pinot Blanc,
    Pinot Noir, or Merlot
Ham – Rosé Vouvray Gewürztraminer
Lamb – Cabernet from Bordeaux,
    Rioja Red from Spain

Pork – Italian or Spanish Red
Veal – California Chardonnay
Lobster – Champagne, Dry Reisling
    or White Burgundy
Oysters – Muscadet, Chablis or Champagne
Shrimp – Light and dry white wine
Swordfish – White wine
Tuna – Versatile like chicken; anything
    but a big red is okay

This is only a partial listing of their recommended matches. Surprising, to me at least, is that May and Sharpe claim that no wine is a good match with chocolate. Yet I (and others I know) have found old Cabernets, Bordeauxs and Ports to be an incredible match. Perhaps they were not eating Godiva chocolate. That I am not alone in my like for the marriage of chocolate and wine is evident by the Chocolate and Wine Festival in Seneca Lakes, New York, held every February in the weekend closest to Valentines Day. This two day event is dedicated to the tasting of chocolate and wine as the ultimate symbiotic, gastronomical fete.

My favorite wine and food match is (the reasonably priced) Rosso di Montalcino or Vino Nobile di Montepulciano with Italian sausage, roasted with peppers, mushrooms, onions, garlic and pine nuts.

Numerous books have been written about just the pairing of wine and cheese. The classic pairing is wine and cheese from the same terroir. Writing in the *World of Cheese*, in 1976, Evan Jones declared that "there is a natural affinity between two products of the same district," referring to the marriage of artisanal cheese and wine from the same district. A dry, sparkling wine is considered the best choice when you want a single wine to serve with a variety of cheeses.

While wine enhances food, there is a certain culinary physics that makes it clear that different foods will bring out varying flavors in the same wines. Classic pairings of wine and food are revered by culinary experts as are renaissance paintings by art critics. With the palette being the common denominator of both paint and canvas and food and wine creations, the possibilities are infinite. In the November, 2000, *Wine Spectator*, the publisher challenged six of America's greatest chefs to create magical menus, each using the same four wines, with the singular goal of seeing how different foods would bring out varying flavors in the same wines. The results of this culinary mating game and the recipes are published in the November 30, 2000, issue of *Wine Spectator*.

Like any significant pursuit, the matching of wine and food requires practice, providing reason enough to want to become an expert (even if never becoming one). The possibilities for matching wine with food are as infinite as there are recipes and wine labels to be put in combination. Both the traditional rules as well as one's personal taste and experience can form the basis for knowledge derived from enjoyable experimentation. In reality, the pairing process is pseudo-intellectual, highly personal, and unpredictable – if it involved walking, it could be called golf. Like golf, a number of rules beyond "taste and learn" have evolved in the game of pairing wine with food. Some of the basic rules and non-rules are as follows:

1. Opposites attract.
Rich food is good with wine that contains healthy acidity to cut through the fat and cleanse your palate. Salty or spicy food tastes good with wine that has some complementary sweetness.

2. Great minds think alike.
Matching attributes can work as well as contrasting them. Rich food pairs as well with rich wine as with acidic wine. With hearty food, you don't have a choice; it needs full-bodied wine. Similarly, a delicate dish requires light wine, and food with lots of acidity needs equally zesty wine.

3. Double your pleasure.

Mirroring the keynote flavor of food can make a fine pairing. Does that dish have cilantro? Think of herbal-tasting wines like Loire Sauvignon Blanc or Chenin Blanc. If it's peppery, a spicy Rhône wine would work. If it has a fruit sauce, a fruity Zinfandel will do the trick.

4. Tannin needs taming.

Wines such as young Bordeaux or Barolo need protein and fat to counteract their puckeriness.

5. There is wisdom in tradition.

You can rely on history and choose a wine from the same country or region as the cuisine you're serving. Others will have paved the way out of necessity.

6. Red and white rules can be broken.

Salmon and Pinot Noir are a classic match, and pork is great with Pinot Gris. Tannic reds taste intensely metallic when drunk with oily fishes, such as bluefish, mackerel, or sardines. Reds that are low in tannin and high in acidity will mute well.

Unlike a lot of other alcoholic and
non-alcoholic beverages, wine was perfectly meant
to be enjoyed with food as the following passages
make very evident.

There is no meal without wine in my family.
Wine is food, an integral part of our meal.
Jaques Pepin

Avoid peanuts; they destroy wine flavors.
Hugh Johnson
from *Pocket Encyclopedia of Wine*

Dogges of nature doe abhorre wine. Whereof
hath growne that Latine proverb **Caninum**
prandium, *a dogs dinner, where is no wine*
at dinner or supper.
Thomas Cogan, *The Haven of Health*, 1636

Wine goes with food. Wine writers are used
to judging wines without food. That is
suffering, you know.
Angelo Gaga

The primary purpose of wine is to make
food taste better.
Myra Waldo

It is salutary for an Englishman to live for a while in a wine-growing country... where wine is neither a symbol by which snobs can demonstrate their wealth or their taste, nor a means of fuddlement, but as natural and as necessary as bread.
Cyril Ray, *Ray on Wine*

I cook with wine, sometimes I even add it to the food!
Leslie Duncan

Alonso of Aragon was wont to say in commendation of age, that age appears to be best in four things – old wood best to burn, old wine to drink, old friends to trust, and old authors to read.
Francis Bacon from *Apothegms*

An evening without wine is like a day without sunshine.
Italian Proverb

A meal without wine is like a day without sunshine.
Anthelme Brillat-Savarin (1755-1826)

A meal without wine... is breakfast!
Molly Mann, American Entrepreneur

*What contemptible scoundrel stole the cork
from my lunch?*
  W.C. Fields

*It was almost spiced, so sweetly aromatic it was.
It caressed the gullet; it spread its greeting over
all the mouth, until the impatient throat accused
the tongue of unfair delay.*
  Maurice Healy

*To enjoy wine... what is needed is a sense of
smell, a sense of taste and an eye for color.
All else is experience and personal preference.*
  Cyril Ray, *Ray On Wine*

*Have you noticed how bread tastes when you
have been hungry for a long time! ... how
good it was! As for the wine, I sucked it all
down in one draught, and it seemed to go
straight into my veins and flow round my
body like new blood.*
  George Orwell

*Wine is the intellectual part of a meal,
meats are merely the material part.*
  Alexandre Dumas,
  Le Grand Dictionnaire de cuisine, 1873

...distilled dew and honey with the fragrance
of all the fresh wild flowers of the field
greeting the dawn.
  André Simon (1877-1970) on Chateau d'Yquem

I had to cook a dinner glorious enough to
complement the Lafite. It took four days.
  Gael Greene

Never apologize for, or be ashamed of, your
own taste in wine. Preferences for wine vary
just as much as those for art or music.
  Hubrecht Duijker

To say that with soup one has to serve a
Montrachet or a white Hermitage, with fish a
Chablis, Pouilly or Graves, with the roast a
Saint-Julien or Pommard, with game a Château
Laffitte or Chambertin, is certainly very
judicious, but it is inadvisable to make rules on
the subject. While it goes without saying
that a heavier wine should be drunk with a
strong-flavoured dish, the only gradation to
follow in the order of wines is from the good to
the better, for it is realities, not etiquette,
that count... All the rest is literature.
  Maurice des Ombiaux,
  Le Gotha des vins de France, 1925

Wine stimulates the appetite and enhances food.
It promotes conversation and euphoria and can
turn a mere meal into a memorable occasion.
 Derek Cooper

Wine is meant to be with food — that's the
point of it.
 Julia Child

A restaurant's menu should include, for each
wine, at least one dish to show it off,
as well as others that will reveal its least
suspected qualities. And, for each dish, there
should be no less than three or four wines that
can accompany it interchangeably, to
accommodate different tastes, different
interests, and different pockets.
 Gerald Asher

Con pan y vino se anda el camino
[With bread and wine you can walk your road].
 Spanish Proverb

I wonder often what the Vintners buy one half
so precious as the goods they sell.
 Omar Khayyam, *The Rubiyat*

Passion, character, individuality, temperament, and attention to detail – great painters and actors embrace these traits, make them part of their own artistic palate and creations. So do great chefs. And, as I came to understand in Europe, so do great wine makers.
  Robert Mondavi

No man has the right to inflict the torture of bad wine upon his fellow creatures.
  Marcus Clarke
  in *The Peripatetic Philosopher*, 1869

One not only drinks wine, one smells it, observes it, tastes it, sips it and one talks about it.
  Edward VII

A rich meal without wine is like an expensive automobile equipped with hard rubber tires.
  Roy Louis Alciatore

Wine is the most extraordinary thing. It is easy but carelessly insulting to take it for granted. It not only offers a wider range of sensations than any other single food or drink, it is also one of the few things we buy that is capable of not just changing, but of changing for the better.
  Janice Robinson from *Vintage Timecharts*, 1989

I am certain that the good Lord never intended perfectly good grapes to be made into jelly.
    Fiorello La Guardia

Wine is a living liquid containing no preservatives. Its life cycle comprises youth, maturity, old age, and death. When not treated with reasonable respect it will sicken and die.
    Julia Child

This wine should be eaten, it is too good to be drunk.
    Jonathan Swift, *Polite Conversation*

A hard drinker, being at table, was offered grapes for dessert. "Thank you," said he, pushing the dish away from him, "but I am not in the habit of taking my wine in pills."
    Anthelme Brillat-Savarin,
    The Physiology of Taste

There is one only course to pursue if you wish to taste the best wines of France... It is to ask the proprietor of any restaurant in which you may eat, what wines he suggests should go with the dishes you have ordered.
    Ford Madox Ford, *Provence*

Fish to taste right must first swim three times:
in water, in butter and in wine.
Anonymous

I have always said drink what you like;
like what you drink. Very simple. This is what
I've been advocating all the time. And the
trouble is, we complicate it with food.
Robert Mondavi

Chapter III

Wine and Friendship

When people are together, adding wine to the human caldron creates a convivial atmosphere distinct and unmatched without it. Cicero, in his dissertation on *Friendship*, 44 B.C., advises us that "friendship makes prosperity more shining and lessens adversity by dividing and sharing it."

Wine has been an essential part of most great cultures, and the enjoyment of wine is an international language that can cross barriers of tradition, religion, and nationality. Thus, the reliable truth of Jaques Pepin who opined: "The suspicious foreigner always looks more gentle and convivial over a glass of wine."

Like a good book find, people like to share good wine with friends. Sharing wine with friends is extolled as one of the high pleasures of drinking wine in the passages that follow in this section.

Friendship is the wine of life. Let's drink of it and to it.
   Anonymous

Wine to me is passion. It's family and friends. It's warmth of heart and generosity of spirit. Wine is art. It's culture. It's the essence of civilization and the art of living.
   Robert Mondavi
   from autobiography *Harvests of Joy*

The great point about really fine wines is that one cannot drink them with any pleasure by one's self.

George Rainbird

'Have some wine,' the March Hare said in an encouraging tone. Alice looked all around the table, but there was nothing on it but tea. 'I don't see any wine,' she remarked. 'There isn't any,' said the March Hare. 'Then it wasn't very civil of you to offer it,' said Alice angrily.

Lewis Carroll

The best use of bad wine is to drive away poor relations.

French Proverb

When wine enlivens the heart, may friendship surround the table.

Anonymous

Last week, I had to offer my publisher a bottle that was far too good for him, simply because there was nothing between the insulting and the superlative.

A.J. Liebling, *Between Meals*

There must always be wine and fellowship or we are truly lost.

Ann Fairbairn

*When thou comest into thy neighbor's vineyard,
then thou mayest eat grapes thy fill at thine
own pleasure; but thou shalt not put any
in that vessel.*
> The Bible, Deuteronomy 23:24

*In water one sees one's own face; but in wine,
one beholds the heart of another.*
> French Proverb

*Dinner parties were problems because I was
always explaining myself. No, I don't drink,
thank you. Not even wine? Nothing, thanks.
But why? I have no talent for it, I said.*
> Pete Hamill

*I drank a bottle of wine for company. It was
Chateau Margaux. It was pleasant to be
drinking slowly and to be tasting the wine
and to be drinking alone. A bottle of wine
was good company.*
> Ernest Hemingway from *The Sun Also Rises*

*A bottle of wine begs to be shared; I have never
met a miserly wine lover.*
> Clifton Fadiman

He fetch'd me gifts of varied excellence;
Seven talents of fine gold; a book all framed
Of massy silver; but his gift most prised
Was twelve great vessels, fill'd with
    such red wine
As was incorruptible and divine.
    Homer, *The Odyssey*,
    George Chapman's translation

Be careful to trust a person who
does not like wine.
    Karl Marx

Always hurry the bottle round for five or six
rounds without pressing yourself or permitting
others to propose. A slight fillip of wine
inclines people to be pleased and removes
the nervousness which prevents men from
speaking — disposes them in short to be
amusing and to be amused.
    Sir Walter Scott, *Journal*, February 22, 1827
    (advice on speaking in public at a dinner)

May friendship, like wine, improve as time
advances and may we always have old wine,
old friends, and young cares.
    Anonymous

Teetotalers lack the sympathy and generosity of men that drink.
W. H. Davies

The wine cellar, like the wedding oath, 'for richer, for poorer...', is a commitment. That commitment is to bring together as many interesting and pleasure-giving bottles of wine as possible and to share those pleasures with family and friends.
William I. Kaufman,
Letts Wine Cellar and Label Book

Never press wine on a guest; it is ill-mannered.
Cyrus Redding, 'Wine Sayings of My Uncle,'
Every Man His Own Butler, 1839

A thousand cups of wine do not suffice when true friends meet, but half a sentence is too much when there is no meeting of minds.
Chinese Proverb

What is better than to sit at the end of the day and drink wine with friends, or substitutes for friends?
James Joyce

May you never want for wine, nor for a friend to help drink it.
French Proverb

The gastronome is less concerned with the vintage than with knowing if the wine is ready for drinking. It does not mean that one does not like to know the provenance and status of the wine, but the host who thinks it amusing to make his guests guess name and year is childish.
    Maurice des Ombiaux,
    Le Gotha des vins de France, 1925

I like best the wine drunk at the cost of others.
    Diogenes

The soft extractive note of an aged cork being withdrawn has the true sound of a man opening his heart.
    William Samuel Benwell

It is a deadly insult to refuse to take a drink from a man, unless an elaborate explanation and apology be given and accepted.
    M. J. F. McCarthy

Wine makes a man better pleased with himself... but the danger is, that while a man grows better pleased with himself, he may be growing less pleasing to others.
    Samuel Johnson
        Note: This is also found as
        Wine makes a man more pleased with himself;
        I do not say it makes him more pleasing to others.

From wine what sudden friendship springs.
John Gay (1688-1732)

*Sir Joshua said... that a moderate glass enlivened
the mind, by giving a proper circulation to the
blood. 'I am (said he), in very good spirits
when I get up in the morning. By dinnertime I
am exhausted; wine puts me in the same state
as when I got up; and I am sure that moderate
drinking makes people talk better.'*
James Boswell, *Life of Johnson*, April 12, 1776

*Bronze is the mirror of the form; wine,
of the heart.*
Aeschylus (525-456 B.C.)

*Do not force your opinion of a wine down the
throats of your guests. Patiently listen to theirs.
You will have lots of fun.*
Charles Walter Berry, *A Miscellany of Wine*, 1932

*Wine and women will make men of
understanding to fall away.*
The Bible, Apocrypha 19:2

Music is the wine that fills the cup of silence.
Robert Fripp

The last twenty years of the reign of George II, and the ten years of his eldest son, were singularly remarkable for excessive wine drinking... Princes, judges, clergymen, the noblest of the land, rather prided themselves than otherwise on such social excesses. To drink less than two bottles of wine at a dinner table gave a man the character of a milksop. Your steady-going guest was content with three bottles, but if you were a person of mark it was indispensable that you should empty a fourth bottle. Bumper glasses were the rule, and you were expected to fill your glass whenever the decanter came around. The stronger sort of wines were almost invariably used... Mr. Croker in his **Book of Reminiscences**, declared that, when a very young man, being invited to dine with royalty, and knowing that his stomach would not bear the enormous consumption of wine, he provided himself with a large sponge, and secreting it in his napkin, returned the wine from his mouth to the sponge, and rid himself of the accumulation by squeezing it under the table.

Charles Tovey,
Wit, Wisdom and Morals Distilled from Bacchus, 1878

One last word: Never let a drunkard choose
your wine. You may be sure he knows nothing
about it. It is only sober people who know
how to drink.

    M. Constantin-Weyer

The wines were chiefly port, sherry and hock;
claret and even Burgundy being then designated
'poor, thin, washy stuff'. A perpetual thirst
seemed to come over people, both men and
women, as soon as they had tasted their soup;
as, from that moment, everybody was taking
wine with everybody else till the close of the
dinner; and such wine as produced that class of
cordiality which frequently wanders into
stupefaction. How all this sort of eating and
drinking ended was obvious, from the
prevalence of gout.

    Captain R.H. Gronow,
    Reminiscences and Recollections, 1810-1860

To buy very good wine nowadays requires
only money. To serve it to your guests is a
sign of fatigue.

    William F. Buckley, *Harpers Bazaar*, Sept. 1979

So life's years begin and closes;
Days though shortening still can shine;
What though youth gave love and roses,
Age still leaves us friends and wine.

National Airs (1815). *Spring and Autumn*, Stanza I

Drinke first a good large draught of Sallet Oyle,
for that will floate upon the wine which you
shall drinke, and supresse the spirites from
ascending into the braine. Also what quantitie
soeuer of newe milke you drinke first you may
well drinke thrise as much wine after, without
daunger of being drunke. But howe sicke you
shall bee with this preuention, I will not heere
determine, neither woulde I have set downe this
experiment, but openly for the helpe of such
modest drinkers as sometimes in companie are
drawne, or rather forced to pledge in full bolles
such quaffing companions as they would
be loth to offend.

Sir Hugh Plat,
The Jewell House of Art and Nature, 1594

An invitation to 'come over for a glass of
sherry' promises a relaxed communion of
friends, comfortable shoes, an old sweater,
an occasion that no one will be using as part
of life's strategic game plan.

Gerald Asher

All [wine's] associations are with occasions when people are at their best; with relaxation, contentment, leisurely meals and the free flow of ideas.
Hugh Johnson

As Brillat-Savarin said: 'Entertaining a guest means you take charge of his happiness for the whole time he is with you.' What better way to treat a guest than to drink wine together slowly, and with friends.
Henry McNulty from *Vogue A-Z of Wine*

The wines that one remembers best are not necessarily the finest that one has tasted, and the highest quality may fail to delight so much as some far more humble beverage drunk in more favourable surroundings.
H. Warner Allen from *A Contemplation of Wine*

When asked what wine he liked to drink, he replied, 'That which belongs to another.'
Diogenes Laërtius

For, like friends the fascinating thing about wine is that no two bottles are exactly alike.
William I. Kaufman,
Letts Wine Cellar and Label Book

Friends and wine must be old.
(Amice e vino devono essere vecchi).
Italian Proverb

Forsake not an old friend, for the new is not
comparable unto him. A new friend is as new
wine: when it is old thou shalt drink it with
pleasure.
The Bible, Ecclesiasticus 9:10

Chapter IV

Wine and
the Good Life

Once a society has mastered sustenance and shelter, its members have the time and inclination to pursue the sheer enjoyment of life. The cultivation and consumption of wine have been significant in taking us beyond the basics of living and to the "good life." Drinking wine for the pure enjoyment of it has always been part of the "good life." It is indicative not only of the means to obtain the wine, but also of having the time to enjoy it beyond the time needed for the basic requirements of life, although many of the sources in this section would no doubt consider wine a basic requirement of life.

Wine makes every meal an occasion, every table more elegant, every day more civilized.
　　Andre Simon

Man doth not live by bread only.
　　The Bible, Deuteronomy 8:3

I think wine has taken over from the toys of the old days like watches and cars. Wine shows you have money, but it also shows you have taste.
　　Thomas Matthews

Never spare the parson's wine nor the baker's pudding.
　　Benjamin Franklin

*There is nothing like wine for conjuring up
feelings of contentment and goodwill. It is
less of a drink than an experience, an
evocation, a spirit. It produces sensations
that defy description.*
  Thomas Conklin from *Wine, A Primer*

Life is too short to drink bad wine.
  Sharon Tyler-Herbst

*Some take their gold in minted mold, and some
in harps hereafter, but give me mine in red wine
and keep the change in laughter.*
  Oliver Herford, loosely

*The wine market is a market of pleasure,
deluxe. It is not a first necessity.*
  Simon Loftus, Quoting Pierre Coste, a Bordeaux
  negociant in *Anatomy of the Wine Trade*

*Towards evening, about supper-time, when
the serious studies of the day are over, is the
time to take wine.*
  Clement of Alexandria, *Paedagogus II*

*In the luxuriance of a bowl of grapes set out in
ritual display, in a bottle of wine, the soil and
sunshine of California reached millions for
whom that distant place would henceforth be*

envisioned as a sun-graced land resplendent
with the goodness of the fruitful earth.
    Kevin Starr, *Inventing the Dream:*
    California Through the Progressive Era

A man hath no better thing under the sun,
than to eat, and to drink, and to be merry.
    The Bible, Ecclesiastes 8:15

The most important reason for starting a wine
cellar, expanding a wine cellar or just having a
wine cellar is the enrichment of one's life,
through the process of learning. Let's face it,
a mere collection of bottles that you have no
knowledge of is like having friends that you say
little to and never exchange ideas with.
    William I. Kaufman,
    Letts Wine Cellar and Label Book

Drink wine, and live here blitheful while ye
may; The morrow's life too late is, live today.
    Robert Herrick

How simple and frugal a thing is happiness: a
glass of wine, a roasted chestnut, a wretched
little brazier, the sound of the sea... All that is
required to feel that here and now happiness
is a simple, frugal heart.
    Nikos Kazantzakis

Wine exalts the fantasy, makes the memory
lucid, increases happiness, alleviates pain,
destroys melancholy. It reconciles dreams,
comforts old age, aids convalescence and gives
that sense of euphoria by which life is made
to run smoothly, tranquilly and lightly.
    Jack D. L. Holmes

On foreign mountains may the sun refine
The grape's soft juice, and mellow it to wine,
With citron groves adorn a distant soil,
And the fat olive swell with floods of oil.
    Joseph Addison

Wine is a friend, wine is a joy; and,
like sunshine, wine is the birthright of all.
    André Simon

Time means so much in the life of a fine wine,
that Time should not be stinted in its
appreciation. The wine of pedigreed lineage is
poured to be courted and played with − not
instantly tossed down the throat.
    H. Warner Allen

If food is the body of good living,
wine is its soul.
    Clifton Fadiman

To fully relish the experience of wine you must wallow in it like a child in the mud...
No pretensions, simply a joy ride of the senses. Wallow away.
  Greg Brown, Winemaker

In Bordeaux, as in the rest of France, the marriage of food and wine is celebrating hundreds of years of happiness. If there is relatively little thrill or experimentation, well, that's the way it often is with successful long-term marriage. But there's plenty of the ease, comfort and pleasure of partners content with each other.
  Florence Fabricant

It's a privilege to drink good wine.
We should treat it with respect and savor every drop, like experts.
  Ralph Steadman

The king can drink the best of wine –
* So can I;*
And has enough when he would dine –
* So have I;*
And can not order rain or shine –
* Nor can I;*
Then where's the difference – let me see –
Betwixt my lord the king and me?
  Charles Mackay

A man, fallen on hard times, sold his art
collection but kept his wine cellar. When asked
why he did not sell his wine, he said, 'A man
can live without art, but not without culture.'
Anonymous

Five qualities are wine's praise advancing:
Strong, beautiful, fragrant, cool and dancing.
John Harrington

A cellar without wine, a home without woman,
and a purse without money, are the
three deadly plagues.
Cyrus Redding, 'Wine Sayings of My Uncle,'
Every Man His Own Butler, 1839

Buying a winery here is like buying a piece
of fine art. It's like purchasing a
Rembrandt or Picasso.
Anonymous

I beg you come tonight and dine
A welcome waits you and sound wine
The Roederer chilly to a charm
As Juno's breasts the claret warm...
T.B. Aldrich

Wine drunken with moderation is the joy of the
soul and the heart.
The Bible, Ecclesiasticus: 31:36

*Wine is one of the most civilized things in the
world and one of the most natural things of the
world that has been brought to the greatest
perfection, and it offers a greater range
for enjoyment and appreciation than, possibly,
any other purely sensory thing which
may be purchased.*
  Ernest Hemingway

*There is no money, among that which I have
spent since I began to earn my living, of the
expenditure of which I am less ashamed, or
which gave me better value in return, that the
price of the liquids chronicled in this book.
When they were good, they pleased my senses,
cheered my spirits, improved my moral and
intellectual powers, besides enabling me to
confer the same benefits on other people.*
  George Saintsbury, *Notes on a Cellar-Book*, 1920

*Baths, wine and Venus bring decay to our
bodies. But baths, wine and Venus make
life worth living.*
  Epitaph on Latin Fountain

*Wine is the sort of alcoholic beverage that does
not destroy but enriches life; does not distort but
clarifies perspective; does not seduce except in a
way which humans should be seduced.*
  Bill St. John

Never buy the cheapest wine in any category, as
its taste may discourage you from going on.
The glass, corks, cartons and labor are about
the same for any wine, as are the ocean freight
and taxes for imported wines. Consequently, if
you spend a little more, you are likely to get a
better wine, because the other costs remain
fixed. Cheap wine will always be too expensive.
  Alex Bespaloff found in
  New Signet Book of Wine

Wine of California... inimitable fragrance and
soft fire... and the wine is bottled poetry.
  Robert Louis Stevenson (1850-1894)

Musigny is a wine of silk and lace.... Smell the
scents of a damp garden, the perfume of a rose,
the violet bathed in morning dew.
  Gaston Roupnel

The point of drinking wine is... to taste sunlight
trapped in a bottle, and to remember some stony
slope in Tuscany or a village by the Gironde.
  John Mortimer

At the end of the day, wine is entertainment.
You share it like a movie or an opera, with
friends.
  Francis Ford Coppola

This song of mine
is a song of the vine
To be sung by the glowing embers
of wayside inns,
When the rain begins
to darken the Drear November.
    Henry Wadsworth Longfellow

Reminds me of my safari in Africa. Somebody
forgot the corkscrew and for several days we
had to live on nothing but food and water.
    W. C. Fields

Never drink bad wine out of compliment;
self-preservation is the first law.
    Charles Tovey,
    Wit, Wisdom and Morals Distilled from Bacchus, 1878

Wine was created from the beginning to make
men joyful, and not to make them drunk.
    The Bible, Ecclesiastes 31

Let us give wine – its selection, care and
tasting – all the attention it deserves, but we
should not become like certain gastronomes
who make a mystery of it, only accessible
to the initiated.
    Pierre Andrieu, Les Vin de France, 1939

Wine has been the foremost of luxuries to millennia of mankind.
    Hugh Johnson, *The Story of Wine*

Wine, the most delightful of drinks, whether we owe it to Noah, who planted the vine or Bacchus, who first pressed juice from the grapes, dates from the childhood of the world.
    Anthelme Brillat-Savarin,
    The Physiology of Taste, 1826

Whatever its price may be, wine surely is worth more than the money that it costs to buy when it brings joy to your home, the joy of sunshine.
    André Simon, *How to Enjoy Wine*

Wine is the most civilized thing in the world.
    Ernest Hemingway

...drinking good wine with good food in good company is one of life's most civilized pleasures.
    Michael Broadbent

Variety is the spice of life, and drinking different wines inevitably makes life more interesting.
    Anthony Meisel and Sheila Rosenzweig,
    American Wine, 1983

Give me a bowl of wine,
I have not that alacrity of spirit,
Nor cheer of mind, that I was wont to have.
William Shakespeare, *Richard III*

Bacchus opens the gates of the heart.
Horace, *Satires I.iv.*

This wine is too good for toast-drinking,
my dear. You don't want to mix emotions up
with a wine like that. You lose the taste.
Ernest Hemingway, *The Sun Also Rises*

Wine glasses, like fine wines, have always been
a symbol of civilized living. The finest glasses
are large and tulip-shaped, clear and thin,
without markings, the bowl the size of a large
orange or an apple. When less than half filled,
such a glass permits the full enjoyment of the
color, bouquet, and taste of a fine wine.
Alexis Lichine

It is difficult to enjoy a good wine
in a bad glass.
Evelyn Waugh, *Wine in Peace and War*

A person with increasing knowledge and sensory
education may derive infinite enjoyment
from wine.
Ernest Hemingway

Go, little book, and wished wall,
Flowers in the garden, meet in the hall,
A bin of wine, a spice of wit,
A house with lawns enclosing it,
A living river by the door,
A nightingale in the sycamore!
Underwoods (1887), *Envoy*

...one of the elegant extras of life.
Charles Dickens

If all be true that I do think,
There are five reasons we should drink:
Good wine − a friend − or being dry −
or lest we should be by and by −
or any other reason why.
John Sirmond (also erroneously ascribed to
Henry Aldrich, *Five Reasons for Drinking,*
in the Biographia Britannica, 2nd Ed.)

With years a richer life begins,
The spirit mellows:
Ripe age gives tone to violins,
Wine, and good fellows.
John Townsend Trowbridge (1827-1916),
Three Worlds

I cried for madder music and for stronger wine.
    Ernest Dowson (1867-1900)

Overlook the madness taking over me,
which, after all, is just the result of loving thee -
silence my contortions with your remedy
and drown this eulogizing in wine's camaraderie!
    Anonymous

Time spent drinking wine is not subtracted
from one's lifespan.
    Gaudeamus Igitur

The bouquet of wine comes like a sunbeam,
and must be enjoyed at the moment.
    Cyrus Redding, 'Wine Sayings of My Uncle,'
    Every Man His Own Butler, 1839

Wine moistens and tempers the spirits, and lulls
the cares of the mind to rest.... It revives our
joys and is oil in the dying flame of life. If we
drink temperately, and small draughts at a time,
the wine distills into our lungs like sweetest
morning dew.... It is then the wine commits no
rape upon our reason but pleasantly invites us
to agreeable mirth.
    Attributed to Socrates by Joni G. McNutt in
    In *Praise of Wine*

If your heart is warm with happiness,
you'll need a glass — if sorrow chills your
heart, have two!
    Hannu Lehmusvuori

By making this wine vine known to the public,
I have rendered my country as great a service as
if I had enabled it to pay back the national debt.
    Thomas Jefferson

Compromises are for relationships, not wine.
    Sir Robert Scott Caywood

I was no more than three when my father... gave
me a full liqueur glass of a reddish-brown wine
sent to him from his native Southern France;
the Muscat Wine of Frontignan. It was like a
sun-stroke, or love at first sight.
    Collette, Prisons et paradis

Wine is the drink of the gods, milk the drink
of babes, tea the drink of women, and water
the drink of beasts.
    John Stuart Blackie

The man who likes wine is never a drunkard:
his pleasure is not the senseless consumption of
quantity, but the intelligent anticipation and
appreciation of quality.
    X. M. Boulestin

Come, they say, let us get wine, let us fill
ourselves with strong drink; and tomorrow will
be like this day, great beyond measure.
The Bible, Isaiah 56:12

Wine is earth's answer to the sun.
Margaret Fuller

Amarone... a wine of incredible depth, bouquet
and breed. Forget about that, however, and
listen to the name – preferably pronounced by
Luciano Pavarotti – Am-mahr-roh-nay;
a siren song, a seduction.
Leonard Bernstein,
The Official Guide to Wine Snobbery

A man who could sit under the shade of his own
vine with his wife and his children about him
and the ripe clusters hanging within their reach
in such a climate as this and not feel the highest
enjoyment, is incapable of happiness.
James Busby

Wherever people have chosen to settle and live,
they have first of all made quite sure that there
was a supply of water, but whenever they have
attained a higher measure of civilization or
culture, they have always spent a good deal of

73

their time, labour and hard-earned money that they and theirs might drink wine.
    André Simon, *How to Enjoy Wine*

The taste of a good wine is remembered long after the price is forgotten.
    Hubrecht Duijker, *Wine Wisdom*

Only the first bottle is expensive.
    French Proverb

Whether businessmen of the Twentieth Century, bankers of the Nineteenth, thinkers of the Eighteenth, princes of the Seventeenth – and even Adam and Eve – careworn people have always found succour in the natural rhythms of a vineyard. Each year the roots dig deeper to produce wines of increasing complexity which in bottle will mature for another generation, immune to all the madness which Man seems condemned to create for himself.
    Peter Sichel

To pontificate, to let opinions rule your appreciation of wine and to be unable to feel, as the candles gutter and the moon rises on the table, however unsung and lacking in renown, is, for that short moment, perfection itself, is to miss the whole heart of wine – and of life too.
    Oz Clarke

74

Every glass of wine we drink represents a whole year of vineyard cultivation and perhaps several years of effort in the winery.... Yet most of us throw it away, straight down our throats, without even trying to 'read' it.
Janice Robinson

Boy, bring wine and dice. Let tomorrow seek its own salvation! Death, twitching the ear, cries: 'Enjoy your life: I come!'
Virgil from *The Copa*, 23 B.C.

Lazarus, you are more indebted to wine than to your father, for he gave you life but once, while wine has given it back to you a thousand times.
Spanish Source (16th Century), found in
Wine Quotations by Helen Exley

The benefits of wine are manifold from the physical to the philosophical.
Anonymous

I feast on wine and bread, and feasts they are.
Michelangelo (1475-1564)

Grudge myself a good wine? As soon grudge my horse corn.
William Makepeace Thackery

*Wine enhances every meal ... but to the French,
wine enhances life itself.*
Andre L. Simon

*To Italians, the only wrong wine is no
wine at all.*
Anonymous

*And they went into the fields, and gathered their
vineyards, and trod the grapes, and made merry.*
The Bible, Judges 9:27

Chapter V
Wine and Health

As you will see from the passages in this section, the consumption of wine has been linked to a healthy lifestyle for eons. Numerous studies have concluded that there is a reduced incidence of cardiovascular disease and ischemic stroke among moderate wine drinkers – one to two glasses of red wine on a daily basis. Wine causes a slight lowering of the blood pressure as alcohol dilates blood vessels, which in turn reduces blood resistance. It was not, however, until the early 1990s when the American Heart Association publicly acknowledged a number of reputable studies concluding that drinking one to two glasses of red wine per day had demonstrable cardiovascular benefits. Professor Serge Renaud of the French National Institute for Health, in a 1991 survey, found that red wine is the most effective drug yet discovered for the prevention of heart disease. The survey was investigating why the French have a low incidence of heart disease although they do not deprive themselves of pâtes, sauces and cheeses.

Numerous reputable scientific studies give reliable evidence that red wine drinkers enjoy healthier lives. The health hallmark of red wine is its antioxidant property derived from polyphenols. That is why numerous studies have shown red wine to be a statistically distinct winner over the common denominator ethanol found in white wines, beer, and distilled spirits. At the 2001 annual meeting of the European Society for Clinical Investigation, Italian scientist Serenella Rotondo presented the results of her studies of rats fed a high cholesterol diet for six months. Along with this diet, in separate groups the rats were also given red wine, white wine, ethyl alcohol or water (unlucky control group). Then all were induced with a blood clot or thrombosis in the abdominal aorta. Compared with those rats on the water diet, the rats who consumed red wine with their cholesterol laden diets saw blood clotting reduced by 60 percent, and the white wine and alcohol groups had an insignificant reduction. Rotondo's work confirms what is known as the "French Paradox," a phenomenon given epidemiological validation by French researcher Serge Renaud. His initial published work in 1992 found in the English medical journal *The Lancet* explains how the untoward effects of the French diet high in saturated fats are counteracted by the intake of wine. Initially Renaud was unable to conclude whether or not it was a property other than the alcohol which contained the important factor.

Danish scientist Morton Grønbaek has provided more research data showing that red wine as opposed to other forms of alcohol provides unique health benefits. Mr. Grønbaek's research draws from

data on over 33,000 men and women collected
since 1976 at the Copenhagen Center for
Perspective Population Studies. While previous
studies had found that consumption of alcohol can
decrease the risk of stroke, Mr. Grønbaek's studies
demonstrated that three to five glasses of wine a
day actually reduced the risk of heart and stroke
diseases by 60 percent, A number of respected
medical and scientific journals over the past few
years have reported on Mr. Grønbaek's conclusion
that the health advantages to wine drinkers over
that of beer and distilled spirit drinkers is
scientifically sound.

Based on a 13 year epidemiological research of
elderly residents in Bordeaux, France, Jean-Marc
Orgogozo, Chairman of the Neurology Department
of the University Hospital in Pellegran, France, has
debunked the myth that the elderly were at risk
drinking wine on the hypothesis that their livers
had slowed and their brains were more fragile. Mr.
Orgogozo's study demonstrated that elderly
subjects who kept drinking moderate amounts of
wine enjoyed a 50 percent reduction in the risk of
developing Alzheimer's disease and dementia,
compared with the nondrinkers. In addition to
being widely published in French medical journals,
in 1998 the *American Journal of Epidemiology* felt his
study was worthy of publication.

The Federal Dietary Guidelines starting in 1995 no longer contain the statement that there is "no net health benefit" to drinking alcohol and expressly acknowledged that moderate consumption has been associated with a lower risk of heart disease in some people. A good reference to wine and health was co-authored by David H. Whitten, M.D., entitled *To Your Health: Two Physicians Explore the Health Benefits of Wine.*

As if prevention of heart attack or stroke was not reason enough to have one or two glasses of wine a day, a new study completed in the spring of 2001 at Beth Israel Deconist Medical Center in Boston indicates that modern consumption of alcohol reduces the risk of repeat heart attacks. The findings, published in the Journal of the American Medical Association, acknowledge that previous studies indicated that moderate drinking helps lower the risk of heart disease in the first place, but the researchers set out to determine whether it is safe to drink alcohol after a heart attack. Nearly 2,000 patients from over 45 U.S. medical centers took part in the study. Consumption varied but the luckiest participants began a regimen of drinking wine four days after their initial heart attacks and continued for four years. Some of the unlucky participants were placed on a "light consumption" regimen which was defined as one to seven servings a week and others on what was defined as a moderate intake level of seven to twenty-one glasses a week. At the end of four years, seventeen (17) percent of the nondrinkers died from another heart attack, but among the light drinkers only nine (9) percent died, and among the moderate drinkers only seven (7) percent died.

In the summer of 2000, molecular biologists at the University of North Carolina reported that they uncovered evidence showing that Resveratrol, a substance found in wine, can control a genetic switch that may help in cancer prevention and treatment. While scientists have long suspected that Resveratrol was a major cancer-fighting agent, they were puzzled as to its methodology. The University of North Carolina research has led to the reliable conclusion that Resveratrol promotes the death of cancer cells by inhibiting a particular protein gene known as NF kappa B. When under attack, the body's immune system initiates the NF kappa B gene and once activated the gene protects cells, including cancer cells, from chemical and radiation attack, thus making the cancer cells immune to chemotherapy and other treatments. The UNC scientists found that when they added Resveratrol, NF kappa B deactivated and actually began to kill the cancer cells. The study can be found in the July, 2000 issue of *Cancer Research*. High levels of Resveratrol are found in wine, grapes, raspberries, peanuts and other plants. The February, 2002 issue of the *British Journal of Cancer* outlines the metabolic processes that Resveratrol undergoes once it leaves the wine glass and enters our bodies. According to the study, an enzyme called Cyp1b1, which is found in tumor cells, converts Resveratrol into Piceatannol, a highly toxic agent that destroys cancer cells. Fortunately, this process occurs only within the tumor so it does not harm healthy cells or tissue.

The December, 2001 issue of *Nature* has the preliminary research data of London-Base Scientists which has reached a preliminary conclusion that the polyphenols in red wine block a peptide that can constrict blood vessels. This research was limited to animals and similar research has not yet been conducted on humans. However, the study's authors, from the Queen Mary University of London, found that red wine slows the production of a peptide called endothelin-1 which is a peptide that helps maintain the normal structure of blood vessels, but in excess, endothelin-1 can result in the formation of fatty deposits that block the normal flow of blood. In this study the research has exposed cultured cow-aorta cells to alcohol-free polyphenol extracts from 23 red wines, four white wines, rosea, and red grape juice. With the red-wine extracts, a decrease in endothelin-1 production could be seen in as little as an hour with a 50 percent drop within six hours. Red grape juice also inhibited endothelin-1, but was "markedly less potent than red wine." The white wines and the rosea had no effect. This is perhaps the singular study that shows that it is indeed red wine that is the winner among all alcoholic beverages in that its unique combination makes it superior to other forms of alcohol or red grapes. The higher the polyphenol content of the wine, the lower the production was of endothelin-1. Notably, cabernet sauvignon based wines had the highest levels of polyphenols and the biggest effect on reducing the production of peptide or endothelin-1.

Elias Castanas, a professor of experimental endocrinology at the University of Crete School of Medicine, has found evidence suggesting that drinking one or two glasses of red wine per day might inhibit breast and prostrate cancer. Because the results of his tests not only support similar anecdotal and intuitive evidence, the *Journal of Cellular Biochemistry* published the results of his scientific work, a paper entitled "Potent Inhibitory Action of Red Wine Polyphenols on Human Breast Cancer Cells." The respected journal *Nutrition and Cancer* published another paper written by Mr. Castanas entitled "Wine Antioxidant Polyphenols

Inhibit the Proliferation of Human Prostrate Cancer Lines." While Mr. Castanas and his colleagues have only studied cells and not humans, there is clear reproducible, scientific evidence that cancer cells are inhibited by wine. This is not to say that wine cures breast or prostrate cancer, but it is evidence that wine may be a cancer cell inhibitor at different stages of their evolution, and while science is still several years away from proving whether wine's antioxidant polyphenols do kill breast and prostrate cancer cells in humans, preliminary animal studies based on solid science have given unwavering promise for similar effects in humans.

Moderation seems to be the key. Moderate drinking for younger adults is defined as no more than two drinks a day for men and no more than one drink a day for women. For healthy men and women over the age of 65, many health experts suggest that that amount be cut in half. What is "a drink"? It is 12 grams of pure alcohol, the amount found in a 12 oz. beer, a 5 oz. glass of wine, or a shot of 80 proof distilled liquor.

If self-diagnosis has any value, then we must add to the scientific research on the health benefits of red wine the comments of Antonio Todde, an Italian living in the Isle of Sardinia, who died just several days shy of his 113th birthday. Mr. Todde is in the *Guinness Book of Records* as the world's oldest man. On his 112th birthday, Mr. Todde let the world in on the secret to his long life: "Just love your brother and drink a good glass of red wine every day."

The association of wine with health in the words of wisdom in this section, while not the product of medical study or laboratory beaker, are no doubt equally reliable prescriptions.

Nothing is more useful than wine for strengthening the body and also more detrimental to our pleasures if moderation be lacking.
    Pliny the Elder

Wine makes daily living, less hurried, easier with fewer tensions and more tolerance.
    Ben Franklin

Wine has a drastic, an astringent taste. I cannot help wincing as I drink. Ascent of flowers, radiance and heat, are distilled here to a fiery, yellow liquid. Just behind my shoulder-blades some dry thing, wide-eyed, gently closes, gradually lulls itself to sleep. This is rapture. This is relief.
    Virginia Woolf, *The Waves*

*Let us get up early to the vineyards; let us
see if the vine flourish, whether the
tender grape appear.*
　　The Bible, Solomon 7:12

*The juice of the grape is the liquid quintessence
of concentrated sunbeams.*
　　Thomas Love Peacock

*Late morning sleep, wine at midday, chatting
with children, and sitting in the meeting houses
of the ignorant drive a man from this world...
Eight things are beneficial in small amounts but
harmful in excess: bloodletting, business,
cohabitation, sleep, warm water, wealth,
wine, and work.*
　　Talmud, Aboth de Rabbi Nathan

*Wine nourishes, refreshes, and cheers....
Wherever wine is lacking, medicines
become necessary.*
　　The Talmud

*Drink a glass of wine after your soup and you
steal a ruble from the doctor.*
　　Russian Proverb

*Dr. Johnson recommended to me, as he had
often done, to drink water only: 'For (said he),
you are then sure not to get drunk; whereas if
you drink wine you are never sure.' I said,
drinking wine was a pleasure which I was
unwilling to give up. 'Why, Sir, (said he), there
is no doubt that not to drink wine is a great
deduction from life; but it may be necessary.'
He however owned, that in his opinion a free
use of wine did not shorten life.*
    James Boswell, *Life of Johnson*, September 19, 1777

*Though small drink or cold water seeme to
quench thirst better than wine because it
moystneth and cooleth more, yet wine being
more agreeable with nature, and or more subtile
substance & operation, is sooner drawne off the
members, and consequently sooner satisfies and
fils the veines, and so quenchth thirst without
any great alteration of the body; whereas water
by the great coldnesse thereof, sodainely
changeth the body from heat to cold, which is a
dangerous thing, as Hippocrates testifieth.*
    Thomas Cogan, *The Haven of Health*, 1636

*What is the definition of a good wine?
It should start and end with a smile.*
    William Sokolin

Mankind... possesses two supreme blessings.
First of these is the goddess Demeter, or Earth,
whichever name you choose to call her. It was
she who gave to man his nourishment of grain.
But after her there came the son of Semele, who
matched her present by inventing liquid wine as
his gift to man. For filled with that good gift,
suffering mankind forgets its grief; from it
comes sleep; with it oblivion of the troubles of
the day. There is no other medicine for misery.
  Euripides, The Bacchae

He who is master of his thirst is master
of his health.
  Old French Proverb

It is singular how few healthy tea-totallers are
to be met with in our ordinary inhabitants of
cities. Glancing back over the many years which
this question has been forced upon the author by
his professional duties, he may estimate that he
has sedulously examined not less than 50,000 to
70,000 persons, including many thousands in
perfect health. Wishing, and even expecting to
find it otherwise, he is obliged to confess that
he has hitherto met with but very few perfectly
healthy middle-aged persons successfully
pursuing any arduous metropolitan calling
under tea-total habits.
  Dr. William Brinton, On Food and its Digestion, 1861

Sorrow can be alleviated by good sleep, a bath and a glass of good wine.
St. Thomas Aquinas

Smooth out with wine the worries of a wrinkled brow.
Horace, *Epistles*

Many and singular are the commodities of Wine: for it is of it selfe, the most pleasant liquor of all other, and was made from the beginning to exhilarate the heart of man. It is a great increaser of the vitall spirits, and a wonderfull restorer of all powers and actions of the body: it very greatly helpeth concoction, distribution, and nutrition, mightily strengtheneth the natural heart, openeth obstructions, discusseth windinesse, taketh away sadnesse, and other hurts of melancholy, induceth boldnesse and pleasant behaviour, sharpneth the wit, abundantly reviveth feeble spirits, excellently amendeth the coldnesse of old age, and correcteth the tetrick qualities, which that age is subject unto; and to speak all in a word, it maketh a man more courageous and lively both in mind and body.
Dr. Tobias Venner, *Via Recta ad vitam Longam,* 1637

The gods made wine the best thing for mortal
man to scatter cares.
  Stasinius of Cyprus, *The Cypria*

The wine had such ill effects on Noah's health
that it was all he could do to live 950 years. Just
nineteen years short of Methuselah. Show me a
total abstainer that ever lived that long.
  Will Rogers

Drink no longer water, but use a little wine for
thy stomach's sake and thine own infirmities.
  The Bible, 1 Timothy 5:23

It is (said the monk) well doctored! Let a
hundred devils jump on to my back if there are
not more old drunkards around than old doctors!
  Rabelais, *Gargantua*

There is no doubt that as a remedy Beaune is
infinitely more pleasant than bicarbonate of
soda, gentian-tonic or even Vichy water.
  Maurice des Ombiaux,
  Le Gotha des Vins de France, 1925

Drinking makes you loquacious, as we all know,
and if what you've got for company is a piece of
paper, then you're going to talk to it. Just try to
enunciate and try to make sense.
  Madison Smart Bell

The art of wine today is a blend of science and technology, as well as the art and intuition of the wine maker. But the essence of great wine remains terroir (meaning soil and climate).
Timothy Mondavi

When a sensible wine-drinker is confronted by scares and panics concerning the horrors of alcohol he remains unmoved, for he knows very well that his trusty beverage is not mere alcohol, but alcohol modified and corrected by the other and more abundant constituents of wine.
C. E. Hawker, Chats About Wine, 1907

From the farmer's simplest homemade potable that I drank as a young person in France to the great wines of the Cotes du Rhone or California, wine has always been a part of my daily repast.
Jaques Pepin

Wine, as a restorative, as a means of refreshment when the powers of life are exhausted, as a means of correction and compensation, where misproportion occurs in nutrition and the organism is deranged in its operation, and as a means of protection against transient organic disturbances, wine is surpassed by no product of nature or art.
Professor Justus Liebig, c.1832

Wine gives strength to weary men.
Homer

More and more, when we talk about good wine,
good food and good friends, we're talking
not just about a gracious lifestyle, but
a healthful one.
R. Michael Mondavi

The City Press quotes a manuscript on
parchment attached to an ancient painting
removed in 1803 from the old Bull Inn,
Bishopgate Street: 'Portrait of Mr. Van Dorn, a
Hamburg merchant. Belonged to a club called
"The Amicable Society", held at the Bull Inn,
Bishopgate Street, for a period of 22 years.
During the above period he drank 35,680 bottles
of wine... averaging at nearly four bottles and a
half per day; and did not miss drinking the
above quantity but two days – the one of which
was the burial of his wife, and the other the
marriage of his daughter, and lived till he was
ninety years of age. Painted by Mr. Hymon,
in the year 1743.'
Charles Tovey,
Wit, Wisdom and Morals Distilled from Bacchus, 1878

Wine is the remedy for the moroseness
of old age.
Plato, 360 B.C.

Place a substantial meal before a tired man and he will eat with effort and be little better for it at first. Give him a glass of wine or brandy, and immediately he feels better: you see him come to life again before you.

Brillat-Savarin (1755-1826)

The secret to a long life is to stay busy, get plenty of exercise, and don't drink too much. Then again, don't drink too little!

Hermann Smith-Johannson

Some time ago I read of fourteen octogenarians living in the little commune of St Julien Beycheville, who, all their lives, had taken their quota of wine (claret), and they joined together to give a celebration of the event, a kind of tribute to Bacchus. Some might regard these as exceptional cases, drinking a bottle of wine daily and living to so great an age. But it is not so. Statistics prove the same in the wine-growing districts of Spain and Portugal, Italy and Greece.

Charles Walter Berry, *A Miscellany of Wine*, 1932

Wine is one of life's most healthful pleasures.

Robert Mondavi

The act of drinking is an act which only races of ancient lineage process. When one makes use of wine moderately, as with all precious things, it is health and medicine. It increases muscular power, it exalts the sex drive, it stimulates the nervous and psychical systems. It renders eloquence easy, it leads to benevolence, to good fellowship, to forgiveness and to heroism.
    Jack D. L. Holmes

Fermentation is correlative with life. Wine is the most healthful and most hygienic of beverages.
    Louis Pasteur (1822-1895)

I am sure of this, that if everybody was to drink their bottle a day, there would be not half the disorders in the world there are now. It would be a famous good thing for us all.
    Jane Austin

The juice of the grape is the liquid quintessence of concentrated sunbeams.
    Thomas Love Peacock

He causeth the grass to grow for the cattle, and herb for the service of man; that he may bring forth food out of the earth; and wine that maketh glad the heart of man.
    The Bible, Psalms 104:15

The red wines of Châteauneuf-du-Pape possess remarkable tonic properties. They diffuse a heat within and ensure a lasting glow which is a gift entirely their own and one which is not due to any greater alcoholic strength than other red wines.

André Simon, *A Wine Primer*

Take care of good wine and good wine will take care of you.

Charles Walter Berry, *A Miscellany of Wine*, 1932

Wine is an old man's milk.

Antonio Perez

There are two reasons for drinking wine: when you are thirsty; to cure it; the other, when you are not thirsty, to prevent it.... Prevention is better than cure.

Anonymous

Boys should abstain from all use of wine until their eighteenth year, for it is wrong to add fire to fire.

Plato, *Laws II*

*Never have a small glass of port, my lad. It
just goes wambling around looking for damage
to do. Have a large glass. It settles down and
does you good.*
   Lord Goddard

The sweet poison of misused wine.
   John Milton, Comus

*After a meal a small glass of brandy is, to my
mind, not so much a luxury as a necessity; it is
a wonderful aid to digestion, and if old and
fine, oh! so delectable!*
   Charles Walter Berry, A Miscellany of Wine, 1932

*Come, come, good wine is a good familiar
creature if it be well used; exclaim no
more against it.*
   Shakespeare, Othello, Act II, S.C. 3

*Other safety measures were also implemented.
Masons working high on the walls were given
leather safety harnesses, and their wine was to
be deluded with a third part of water, a mixture
normally reserved for pregnant women.*
   Ross King, Brunelleschi's Dome (describing the
   dangerous work for the teams of masons who
   had to work on the walls that leaned inward at
   an alarming angle on the dome of Florence's
   magnificent cathedral, Santa Maria del Fiore)

Your stomach is your wine cellar, keep the stock small and cool.
　　Charles Tovey

...the juice which so gladdens the human heart.
　　Cyrus Redding,
　　A History and Description of Modern Wines, 1833

Alcohol is a misunderstood vitamin.
　　P. G. Wodehouse

Wine is sunlight, held together by water.
　　Galileo

For a bad night, a mattress of wine.
　　Spanish Proverb

Nothing is so effective in keeping one young and full of lust as a discriminating palate thoroughly satisfied at least once a day.
　　Angelo Pelligrini, The Unprejudiced Palate

When there is plenty of wine, sorrow and worry take wing.
　　Ovid, The Art of Love, (C.A.D. 8)

It sloweth age, it strengtheneth youth, it helpeth digestion, it abandoneth melancholie, it relisheth the heart, it lighteneth the mind, it quickeneth the spirits, it keepeth and preserveth the head from whirling, the eyes from dazzling, the tongue from lisping, the mouth from snaffling, the teeth from chattering and the throat from rattling; it keepeth the stomach from wambling, the heart from swelling, the hands from shivering, the sinews from shrinking, the veins from crumbling, the bones from aching, and the marrow from soaking.

> Copied by Joseph Lyons from a
> 16th Century manuscript

Penicillin cures, but wines makes people happy.

> Sir Alexander Fleming

I think it is a great error to consider a heavy tax on wines as a tax on luxury. On the contrary, it is a tax on the health of our citizens.

> Thomas Jefferson (1743-1826)

I have lived temperately... I double the doctor's recommendation of a glass and a half of wine a day and even treble it with a friend.

> Thomas Jefferson

*Wine from long habit has become an
indispensable for my health.*
    Thomas Jefferson

*When the wine [made at her chateau] is in the
golden period of effervescing, any sick child in
the village ticketed by the doctor can be brought
to the wine-presses and dipped in. If labeled
'tres malade,' he is dipped in twice.*
    Lillie de Hergermann-Lindencrone,
    In the Courts of Memory

*Wine is an appropriate article for mankind,
both for the healthy body and for
the ailing man.*
    Hippocrates

*In Europe then we thought of wines as
something as healthy and normal a food and
also as a great giver of happiness and well being
and delight. Drinking wine was not a snobbism
nor a sign of sophistication nor a cult; it was as
natural as eating and to me as necessary.*
    Ernest Hemingway, A Moveable Feast

*If penicillin can cure those who are ill, Spanish
sherry can bring the dead back to life.*
    Sir Alexander Fleming (1881-1955)
        Note: Also found as, "Penicillin cures,
        but wine makes people happy."

*I have enjoyed great health at a great age
because everyday since I can remember I have
consumed a bottle of wine except when I have
not felt well. Then I have consumed two bottles.*
A Bishop of Seville, *Legendary*

*So wine-drinking should be encouraged in the
same way that we try all the time to induce
people to be more civilized, to have better
meals, to live a more decent life, to appreciate
better things altogether – it should be
encouraged because it is pleasant and
it is healthy.*
X. M. Boulestin

*I rejoice as a moralist at the prospect of a
reduction of the duties on wine by our national
legislature. No nation is drunken where wine is
cheap, and none sober where the dearness of
wine substitutes ardent spirits as the common
beverage... Fix but the duty... and we can drink
wine here as cheap as we do grog and who will
not prefer it? Its extended use will carry health
and comfort to a much enlarged circle.*
Thomas Jefferson

There is no doubt at all that the most moderate use of wine while eating is the pleasantest and probably the most effective tranquilizer known to medical man.
    Dr. Russell V. Lee

*Wine is at the head of all medicines...
Where wine is lacking drugs are necessary.*
    Babylonian Talmud

Give me wine to wash me clean from the weather-stains of care.
    Ralph Waldo Emerson (1803-1882)

Beverage alcohol is our most valuable medicinal agent — and it is the milk of old age.
    Dr. William Osler (1849-1919)

Wine-drinking is no occult art to be practised only by the gifted few. Indeed, it is not an art at all. It is, or should be, the sober habit of every normal man and woman burdened with normal responsibilities and with a normal desire to keep their problems in perspective and themselves in good health.
    Allan Sichel (1900-1965)
    from *The Penguin Book of Wines*

Wine was given by God, not that we might be drunken, but that we might be sober. It is the best medicine when it has the moderation to direct it. Wine was given to restore the body's weakness not to overturn the soul's strength.

St. Chrysostom (347-407)

Chapter VI

Wine and Inspiration

Cyril Milkin said "love is the triumph of imagination over intelligence." When you look at the quoted passages in this section, you will see that wine has been a catalytic converter of imagination. While alcohol has been known to lower inhibitions, many a great leader and writer have extolled its mind expanding virtues, and so seemingly, wine unlocks not only bodily movements, but mental ones as well.

Wine brings to light the hidden secrets of the soul, gives being to our hope, bids the coward fight, drives dull care away, and teaches new means for the accomplishments of our wishes.
    Horace (65-8 B.C.)

May our wine brighten the mind and strengthen the resolution.
    Anonymous

*Wine... moderately drunken
It doth quicken a man's wits,
It doth comfort the heart.*
    Andrew Boorde, 1562, from *Dietary of Health*

*No wine, no wisdom
Too much wine – the same.*
    Pascal

The wine urges me on, the bewitching wine,
which sets even a wise man to singing and to
laughing gently and rouses him up to dance and
brings forth words which were better unspoken.
Homer, *The Odyssey*, bk. XIV

Wine is a good counselor, a true friend, who
neither bores nor irritates us: it does not
send us to sleep, nor does it keep us awake...
It is always ready to cheer, to help, but not
to bully us.
André Simon

Wine, like the rising sun, possession gains,
And drives the mist of dullness from the brains.
George Crabbe, *The Borough*

Wine has... inspired invention, animated
religion, made men vociferous, nourished
beliefs, kindled wrath, provoked love and lust
and softened hard beds.
London Times, "Wine Merchants Uncorked"

Satisfy your hearts with food and wine, for
therein is courage and strength.
Homer, *The Iliad*

It is better to hide ignorance, but it is hard to do this when we relax over wine.

Heraclitus c. 540 – c. 480 B.C.,
On the Universe, fragment 108

Wine is the good companion of soldiers, it gives them courage.

Edouard Barther

I can truthfully say that since I reached the age of discretion I have consistently drunk more than most people would say was good for me. Nor do I regret it... Often wine has shown me matters in their true perspective, and has, as though by the touch of a magic wand, reduced great disasters to small inconveniences. Wine has lit up for me the pages of literature, and revealed in life romance lurking in the commonplace. Wine has made me bold but not foolish; has induced me to say silly things but not to do them. Under its influence words have often come too easily which had better not have been spoken, and letters have been written which had better not have been sent. But if such small indiscretions standing in the debit column of wine's account were added up, they would amount to nothing in comparison with the vast accumulation on the credit side.

Alfred Duff Cooper

*Nothing makes the future look so rosy as to
contemplate it through a glass of Chambertin.*
    Napoleon Bonaparte

*A peculiar subgenre of the English language...
has flowered wildly in recent years, like some
pulpy jungle plant. It's called Winespeak.*
    Frank J. Prial

*A man will be eloquent if you give
him good wine.*
    Ralph Waldo Emerson, *Representative Men*

*By wine we are generous made;
It furnishes fancy with wings;
Without it we should ne'er have had
Philosophers, poets or kings.*
    Anonymous, *Wine and Wisdom*, 1710

*When a man drinks at dinner he begins to be
better pleased with himself.*
    Plato

*Wine is art, it's culture, it's the essence of
civilization and the art of living. Wine has been
with us for 7,000 years, almost since the dawn
of civilization, and for centuries poets, painters,
musicians, and philosophers have sung its*

praises. Even the Bible applauds its virtues. And wine to me is even more. When I pour a glass of truly fine wine, when I hold it up to the light and admire its color, when I raise it to my nose and savor its bouquet and essence, I know that wine is, above all else, a blessing, a gift of nature, a joy as pure and elemental as the soil and vines and sunshine from which it springs.
Robert Mondavi

It is the only beverage that feeds the body, soul, and spirit of man and at the same time stimulates the mind.
Robert Mondavi

Wine certainly sets the mind alight and sets the wits dancing round the central bonfire of genial emotion. But it is an affair of rosy and capricious illuminations, a sunset of inspiration, a showery sunset with a rainbow that soon departs.
Siegfried Sassoon, *Diaries*, July 7, 1922

No poems can please nor live long which are written by water drinkers.
Horace

Most of the confidence which I appear to feel,
especially when influenced by noon wine, is only
a pretense.

    Tennessee Williams from "I am Widely
    Regarded as the Ghost of a Writer"

In wine there is truth.

    Pliny, *Natural History* XIV.xiv
    (*In vino veritas*, the Latin of Pliny's, has been
    an old Italian proverb. This phrase has also
    been attributed to Theognis as *Wine is want*
    to show the mind of man, Theognis, No. 500,
    and to Plato as meaning the confounding
    of a liar.)

As with new wine intoxicated both, They swim
in mirth, and fancy that they feel Divinity
within them breeding Wings where with to
scorn the earth.

    John Milton, *Paradise Lost IX*

Men do not knowingly drink for the effect
alcohol produces on the body. What they drink
for is the brain-effect; and if it must come
through the body, so much the worse
for the body.

    Jack London

The learned Erasmus, who appears to have been of Anacreon's opinion, that if 'With water you fill up your glass, you will never write anything wise', was extremely fond of Burgundy: a good draught of this generous liquor was, he declared, as new blood in his veins, quickening his pen into brightness and life. He attributed the cure of his gastritis to Beaune wine, and was very desirous to live in that town, '**pour boire**', as he said, its '**vin sain et délicieux**.'

Charles R. Weld, *Notes on Burgundy*, 1869

Our bitterest wine is always drained from crushed ideals.

The Devastator

They [the Persians] are accustomed to deliberate on matters of the highest moment when warm with wine; but whatever they in this situation may determine is again proposed to them on the morrow, in their cooler moments, by the person in whose house they had before assembled. If at this time also it meet their approbation, it is executed; otherwise it is rejected. Whatever also they discuss when sober, is always a second time examined after they have been drinking.

Herodotus (484-424 B.C.)

The ethereal blossoms of spring, the angelic voice of a child, the winsome charm of rare vintage wine — each is enough to make the heart sing.

Anonymous

Although Italy is not large, no other country can match the immensity of its historical impact on the course of Western Civilization, its artistic and scientific achievements, or its contributions to the good things in life. Wine is one of these good things, an important one at that, an integral art of the Italian spirit and temperament, past and present.

Burton Anderson

A mind of the caliber of mine cannot derive its nutriment from cows.

George Bernard Shaw

The best wine... that goeth down sweetly, causing the lips of those that are asleep to speak.

The Bible, Song of Solomon 7:9

Port is not for the very young, the vain and the active. It is the comfort of age and the companion of the scholar and the philosopher.

Evelyn Waugh

When [wines] were good they pleased my
sense, cheered my spirits, improved my moral
and intellectual powers, besides enabling me to
confer the same benefits on other people.
  George Saintsbury, *Notes on a Cellar Book*

The best audience is intelligent, well-educated
and a little drunk.
  Alben W. Barkley (1877-1956)

I carry on mental dialogues with the shoots of
the grapevine, who reveal to me grand thoughts
and to whom I can retell wondrous things.
  Johann Wolfgang Von Goethe

Wine can of their wits the wise beguile,
Make the sage frolic, and the serious smile.
  Alexander Pope, *The Odyssey of Homer*

A writer who drinks carefully is probably a
better writer. The main effect of the grain on
the creative personality is that it provides the
necessary sense of newness and freshness,
without which creative writing does not occur.
  Stephen King

Wine was born, not invented... like an old
friend, it continues to surprise us in new and
unexpected ways.
  Dr. Salvatore P. Lucia

The Spirit of Wine
Sang in my glass, and I listened
With love to his odorous music,
His flushed and magnificent song.
    William Ernest Henly

Excellent wine generates enthusiasm.
And whatever you do with enthusiasm is
generally successful.
    Philippe de Rothschild

Wine brings to light the hidden secrets of the
soul, gives being to our hopes, bids the coward
flight, drives dull care away, and teaches new
means for the accomplishment of our wishes.
    Horace

When by mere legislation, man can stop fruit
from fermenting of its own accord after it falls
to the ground he can talk about a law of
prohibition. The very word destroys its meaning.
You can't prohibit nature.
    E. Temple Thurston

Clearly, the pleasures wines afford are
transitory — but so are those of the ballet, or of
a musical performance. Wine is inspiring and
adds greatly to the joy of living.
    Napoleon Bonaparte

*In vino veritas, said the sage... Before Noah,
men having only water to drink, could not find
the truth. Accordingly... they became
abominably wicked, and they were justly
terminated by the water they loved to drink.
This good man, Noah, having seen that all his
contemporaries had perished by this unpleasant
drink, took a dislike to it; and God, to relieve
his dryness, created the vine and revealed to him
the art of making 'levin.' By the aid of this
liquid he revealed more and more truth.*
    Benjamin Franklin

*(Wine) unlocks secrets, bids hopes be
certainties, thrusts cowards into the fray,
takes loads off anxious hearts, teaches new
accomplishments. The life-giving wine cup...
whom has it not made free even in the
pinch of poverty!*
    Horace

*Wine pours into our mouths, you can smell it,
feel it and drink it. I prefer it to music, flowers
or the heavens.*
    French Folk Song

When wine sinks, words swim.
    Scottish Proverb

[Wine] awakens and refreshes the lurking
passions of the mind, as varnish does the
colours which are sunk in a picture, and brings
them out in all their natural glowings.
  Anonymous

Wine is to the parched mind of man what water
is to the sun-drenched plain. It releases the
brakes of his self-consciousness and softens the
hard-baked crust of dust so that the seeds below
may send forth sweet flowers.
  André Simon

Wine gives courage and makes men
apt for passion.
    Ovid (43 B.C.-A.D. 17)

Ah! bouteille, ma mie,
Pourquoi vous videz-vous?
(Ah, bottle, my friend,
why do you empty yourself?)
    Moliére (1622-1673)

The stimulus of wine is favourable to the play of
invention and to fluency of expression.
  G. C. Lichtenberg

Wine uplifts the soul, inspires the heart and
provokes the intellect.
  Anonymous

Wine has nourished our minds, our spirits and
our health since recorded time.
Anonymous

Writing in my sixty-fourth year, I can truthfully
say that since I reached the age of discretion I
have consistently drunk more than most people
would say is good for me. Nor did I regret it.
Wine has been for me a firm friend and a wise
counsellor. Often... wine has shown me matters
in their true perspective, and has, as though by
the touch of a magic wand, reduced great
disasters to small inconveniences. Wine has lit
up for me the pages of literature, and revealed
in life romance lurking in the commonplace.
Wine has made me bold but not foolish;
has induced me to say silly things but not
to do them.
Duff Cooper, Old Men Forget

You say man learned first to build a fire and
then to ferment his liquor. Had he but reversed
the process we should have no need of flint and
tinder to this day.
Anonymous

Wine drinkers never make good artists.
Gratinos

Quickly, bring me a beaker of wine, so that I may wet my mind and say something clever.
Aristophenes

Chapter VII

Wine and Philosophy

The importance of wine is perhaps best exemplified by its incorporation into many people's philosophy of life. While all of the quotes in the following section are not truly capable of being pigeonholed as strictly philosophical, they do demonstrate that wine is up there with the other mysteries of life about which philosophers and others muse and confuse.

The wines that one remembers best are not necessarily the finest that one has tasted, and the highest quality may fail to delight so much as some far more humble beverage drunk in more favourable surroundings.
H. Warner Allen, *A Contemplation of Wine*, 1950

When you drank it, you felt as if you were in communion with the blood of the earth itself.
Nikos Kazantzakis

See! See! the jolly God appears.
His hand a mighty goblet bears.
With sparkling wine full charg'd it flows.
The sovereign cure of human woes.
Greek Poet Anacreon

Name me any liquid – except our own
blood – that flows more intimately and
incessantly through the labyrinth of symbols we
have conceived to make our status as human
beings, from the rudest peasant festival to the
mystery of the Eucharist. To take wine into our
mouths is to savor a droplet of the river
of human history.
  Clifton Fadiman

Wine is Life.
  Petronius

The juice of the grape is given to him that will
use it wisely, as that which cheers the heart of
man after toil, refreshes him in sickness and
comforts him in sorrow. He who so enjoyeth it
may thank God for his wine-cup as for his daily
bread; and he who abuseth the gift of heaven is
not a greater fool in his intoxication than thou
in thine abstinence.
  Sir Walter Scott

Who after wine, talks of war's hardships
or of poverty?
  Horace (65-8 B.C.)

Wine has been with us since the beginning of civilization. It is the temperate, civilized, sacred, romantic mealtime beverage recommended in the Bible. Wine has been praised for centuries by statesmen, philosophers, poets, and scholars. Wine in moderation is an integral part of our culture, heritage and gracious way of life.

Robert Mondavi

When things are good, buy wine, and when things are bad, buy wine.

William I. Kaufman,
Letts Wine Cellar and Label Book

Making good wine is a skill. Fine wine is an art.

Robert Mondavi

I hardly know wherein philosophy and wine are alike unless it be in this, that the philosophers exchange their ware for money, like the wine merchants; some of them with a mixture of water or worse, or giving short measure.

Walter Pater, Marius the Epicurean,
found in *Bartlett's Quotations*

A bottle of wine contains more philosophy than all the books in the world.

Louis Pasteur

The love of wine may almost be classed with the innate principles of our very being.

Anonymous, *The Wine-Drinker's Manual*, 1830

Wine gives great pleasure, and every pleasure is of itself a good.

Samuel Johnson

With Clarets, as in fact with all wines, the vintage is of far greater importance than the name, however illustrious it may be.
A Bourgeois growth of a good year, for instance, is very much to be preferred to a 'classed' growth of a bad one.

C. E. Hawkyer, *Chats About Wine*, 1907

Wine has been created to make people happy.
Wine drunk at the proper time and in moderation is rejoicing heart and gladness of soul.
Wine drunk to excess leads to bitterness of spirit, to quarrels and stumbling.
Drunkenness increases the anger of a fool to his own heart, reducing his strength and adding wounds.

Sirach 31: 27-30

Take counsel in wine, but resolve
afterwards in water.
   Benjamin Franklin

Despair is vinegar from the wine of hope.
   Austin O'Malley

Wine does not intoxicate men;
men intoxicate themselves.
   Chinese Proverb

Do you remember any great poet that ever
illustrated the higher fields of humanity
that did not dignify the use of wine from
Homer on down?
   James A. McDougall

Wine remains a simple thing,
a marriage of pleasure.
   Andre Tchelistcheff, Winemaker

Love wine like a constant mistress; never abuse
it, and you will find it brings no sorrows.
   Cyrus Redding, 'Wine Sayings of My Uncle,"
   Every Man His Own Butler, 1839

Drink wine, drink poetry, drink virtue.
  Charles Baudelaire

*Then sing as Martin Luther sang. As Dr. Martin
Luther sang: 'who loves not wine, woman and
song, he is a fool his whole lifelong.'*
  W.M. Thackeray

*Up to the age of forty eating is beneficial. After
forty, drinking.*
  The Talmud, 200 B.C.

*All wines are by their very nature full of
reminiscence, the golden tears and red blood of
summers that are gone.*
  Richard Le Gallienne

Wine is the blood of France.
  Louis Bertall, La Vigne, 1878

*Wine in every swivel-chair bestow -
such perfume as gives fence-sitters
  a heady glow
the like to which they will never know
unless you open the tap and let wine flow!*
  Anonymous

No poems can please for long or live that are written by water-drinkers.
    Horace

Wines that, heaven knows when,
Had suck'd the fire of some forgotten sun,
And kept it through a hundred years of gloom.
    Alfred, Lord Tennyson, *The Lover's Tale*

Wine is a bride who brings a great dowry to the man who woos her persistently and gracefully.
    Evelyn Waugh

If a man deliberately abstains from wine to such an extent that he does serious harm to his nature, he will not be free from blame.
    Saint Thomas Aquinas

I drink it when I am happy, and when I am sad. I drink it when I am alone, and I find it indispensable for any social gathering... Otherwise I never touch it, except when I am thirsty.
    Liliane Bollinger

Wine in itself is an excellent thing.
Pope Pius XII

Wine rejoices the heart of man and joy is the mother of all virtues.
Johann Wolfgang von Goethe, 1771

Alcohol is nicissary f'r a man so that now an' thin he can have a good opinion iv himself, ondisturbrd be th' facts.
Finley Peter Dunne

Good wine is a necessity of life for me.
Thomas Jefferson

You yourself, my lord Prior, like to drink of the best. So does any honest man; never does a man of worth dislike good wine; it is a monastical apothegm.
Rabelais

Until one can convince the world that Romanée-Conti is a wine rather than an investment bond, the future is very bleak.
Auberon Waugh, *Burgundy Now and Then*

What is man, when you come to think upon him, but a minutely set, ingenious machine for turning with infinite artfulness, the red wine of Shiraz into urine?

Isak Dineson

Bread is made for laughter, and wine gladdens life, and money answers everything.

The Bible, Ecclesiastes 10:19

If wine disappeared from human production, I believe there would be, in the health and intellect of the planet, a void, a deficiency far more terrible than all the excesses and deviations for which wine is made responsible. Is it not reasonable to suggest that people who never drink wine, whether naïve or doctrinaire, are fools or hypocrites...? A man who drinks only water has a secret to hide from his fellowmen.

Baudelaire

No nation is drunken where wine is cheap, and none sober where the dearness of wine substitutes ardent spirits as the common beverage. Wine brightens the life and thinking of anyone.

Thomas Jefferson

*Those who tarry long over wine, those who go
to try mixed wine. Do not look at wine when it
is red, when it sparkles in the cup and
goes down smoothly.*
The Bible, Proverbs 23:30-31

*God made yeast, as well as dough,
and loves fermentation just as dearly as
he loves vegetation.*
Ralph Waldo Emerson

*Some contend it started the first stable
community life. Early man was nomadic.
Several years are required to develop a producing
vineyard, however, and the anthropologists say
that pursuit of wine marks the change from a
scattered human race to a settled one. It may
well be that man was brewer before baker;
lover of liquor before lover of home.*
Morris E. Shafetz

*Alone in the vegetable kingdom, the vine makes
the true savour of the earth intelligible to man.*
Colette from *Prisons et Paradis*

*Montrachet should be drunk kneeling,
with one's head bared.*
Alexandre Dumas (1802-1870)

*Then wine bottles were brought up, carefully
sealed and labelled. 'FALERNIAN, CONSUL
OPIMIUS, ONE HUNDRED YEARS OLD.' While
we were examining the labels, Trimalchio
clapped his hands. 'Wine has a longer life
than us poor mortals,' he sighed; 'so let us
refresh our palates. Wine is life. I am giving
you real Opimian.'*
    Petronius, The Saatyricon

Wine... the blood of grapes.
    The Bible, Genesis 49:11

*Ah, my Beloved, fill the Cup that clears
Today of past regrets and Future Fears:
To-morrow. Why, To-morrow I may be
Myself with Yesterday's Sev'n thousand Years.*
    From The Rubaiyat of Omar Khayyam

*Ultimately, the appeal of wine lies in its
mystery. Of all agricultural endeavors,
wine extracts something from the Earth that
cannot quite be explained.*
    Matt Kramer

Great wine inspires, impresses, invigorates, and, perhaps most significantly, intrigues.
Janice Robinson

Chapter VIII

Wine and Religion

There is much evidence that wine has been inseparable from most major religions since their origins. The Greeks and Romans incorporated wine into various celebrations to many of their numerous gods. Wine is an integral part of Judaism, with Jewish law requiring "kosher" wine in its Passover rights and other religious ceremonies. "Kosher" is not the result of a wine grape, quality or style. What sets it apart are certain rules dictated by Jewish law. From the time the grapes are crushed until the finished product is bottled, only Sabbath-observant Orthodox jews who themselves keep kosher can be physically engaged in the process. A rabbi must supervise. If the winemaking equipment is not used exclusively for kosher wine, it must be ritually sanitized. Only certified kosher yeast and filtering agents are allowed. (Animal derived substances are prohibited and artificial color and preservatives forbidden.)

As with many things, an exception can most always be found. Islam prohibits alcoholic drinks. "Drinking makes people lose their heads and impedes clear thinking. Even music dulls the mind." Ayatollah Khomeini

As mentioned in the introduction, the Bible has hundreds of references to wine in its stories and teachings. Brad Whittington has written a well researched article entitled "Alcohol and the Bible" which provides immense categorical detail on the references to wine in the Bible, The article's purpose is to demonstrate that Christian denominations, which prohibit the use of alcohol, have no scriptural basis for such a stance and that it is merely a prohibitionist or cultural preference without support in the Bible. The article contains analysis of the over 228 specific references to wine found in the Bible. He makes a sound case that there is absolutely no prohibition against the use of alcohol in the Bible. A synthesis of all of the references led Whittington to conclude that to the contrary, moderate use of alcohol was actually encouraged with caution against overindulgence of it (in keeping with its themes of moderation on many practices).

Indeed, Jesus Christ, upon whose doctrines Christianity is founded, used wine in several ways to impart Christian values and ethics. Perhaps the most profound of which was the fact that Jesus chose wine as an essential part of communion. Jesus also confirms wine's role in celebrations when at the marriage feast at Cana he responds to Mary's request to do something about the host having run out of wine by making an additional 120 to 180 gallons of wine superior to that originally offered the guests at the celebration.

Overall, the scripture writers provide numerous preachings that an abundance of wine is an example of God's blessing while a lack of wine is an example of God's disfavor. The largest number of references capable of being categorized illustrate that wine was an accepted and integral part of culture in biblical times.

Where biblical references to wine are in keeping with the purpose of this work, I have provided them in those chapters in which I felt they most closely fit and not just under this chapter on Wine and Religion.

God made only water, but man made wine.
Victor Hugo

We are now to have a Magnum of 1868, Romanée... My word! there's a wine... What did you say? 'I was making a suggestion that we might all stand in silence for half a minute, glass in hand, to offer heartfelt thanks to the Giver of such good things.'
Charles Walter Berry, *Viniana*

It ought to give pause to the most fanatical teetotaler that the only humans worth saving in the Flood were a family of vintners.
Dr. Bernard Rudofsky

Beer is made by men, wine by God!
  Martin Luther

*The Greeks, Romans, Egyptians all appreciated
wine, and in our Western civilization wine has
long been an integral part of our heritage,
customs and social and religious rights.*
  Robert Mondavi

*If God forbade drinking, would He have made
wine so good?*
  Cardinal Richelieu

*Without the vine and its fruit, the history of
mankind might have been very different.
Certainly, religious ritual would be upended, the
American Revolution might have taken a
different tack, and you and I would be reduced
to drinking Diet Cola with our sole Colbert.*
  Anthony Meisel and Sheila Rosenzweig,
  American Wine, 1983

Religions change, but beer and wine remain.
  Hervey Allen (1889-1949)

*Wine should be enjoyed for the benefits of the
soul and nothing more.*
  Peter Fiducia

*In the holy place shalt thou cause the strong
wine to be poured unto the Lord for
a drink offering.*
    The Bible, Numbers 28:7

*No love that in a family dwells,
    no caroling in frosty air,
Nor all the steeple-shaking bells
Can with this single Truth compare –
That God was Man in Palestine
And lives today in Bread and Wine.*
    John Betjeman

*On this mountain the Lord Almighty will prepare
a feast of rich food for all peoples, a banquet of
meats and the finest of wines.*
    The Bible, Isaiah 25:6

*Wouldn't it be terrible if I quoted some reliable
statistics which prove that more people are
driven insane through religious hysteria than
by drinking alcohol?*
    W.C. Fields

*Wine is proof that God loves us and wants to
see us happy.*
    Anonymous

Wine digesteth food and disperseth care and dispelleth flatulence and clarifieth the blood and cleareth the complexion and quickeneth the body and hearteneth the hen-hearted and fortifieth the sexual power in many, but to name its virtue would be tedious. In short, had not Allah forbidden it, there were nought on the face of the earth to stand in its stead.

Ancient Mohammedan Poet

A man hath no better thing under the sun, than to eat, and to drink, and to be merry.

The Bible, Ecclesiastes 8:15

Drink is in itself a good creature of God, and to be received with thankfulness, but the abuse of drink is from Satan, the wine is from God, but the Drunkard is from the Devil.

Increase Mather

Therefore thou shalt speak unto them this word; Thus saith the LORD God of Israel, Every bottle shall be filled with wine; and they shall say until thee, Do we not certainly know that every bottle shall be filled with wine?

The Bible, Jeremiah 13:12

It was considered symbolic of the blood of Christ, part of the ritual, and one of the good things in life.
Martin Elkort, *The Secret Life of Food*

Good wine makes good blood, good blood causeth good humors, good humors cause good thoughts, good thoughts bring forth good works, good works carry a man to heaven, ergo, good wine carrieth a man to heaven.
James Howell, British writer, 1634

We hear of the conversion of water into wine at the marriage in Cana as a miracle. But this conversion is, through the goodness of God, made every day before our eyes. Behold the rain which descends from heaven upon our vineyards, and which incorporates itself with the grapes, to be changed into wine; a constant proof that God loves us, and loves to see us happy. The miracle in question was only performed to hasten the operation, under circumstances of necessity, which required it.
Benjamin Franklin

Drink wine, and you will sleep well. Sleep, and
you will not sin. Avoid sin, and you will be
saved. Ergo, drink wine and be saved.
    Medieval German Saying Anonymous

If Heaven did not love wine,
Then there would be no wine star in Heaven.
If Earth did not love wine
There would be no wine springs on earth –
Why then be ashamed before Heaven
    to love wine?
Three cups, and one can perfectly understand
    the Great Tao;
A gallon, and one is in accord with all nature.
    Li T'ai Po

Go, eat your bread with enjoyment, and drink
your wine with a merry heart; for God has
already approved what you do.
    The Bible, Ecclesiastes 9:7

And Noah began to be a husbandman, and he
planted a vineyard.
    The Bible, Genesis 9:20

For in the hand of the Lord there is a cup, and
the wine is red.
    The Bible, Psalms 75:8

I searched with my mind how to cheer my body
with wine – my mind still guiding me with
wisdom – and how to lay hold on folly,
till I might see what was good for the sons of
men to do under heaven during the few days
of their life.

    The Bible, Ecclesiastes 2:3

Therefore God give thee of the dew of heaven,
and the fatness of the earth, and plenty of corn
and wine: Let people serve thee, and nations
bow down to thee; be lord over thy brethren,
and let they mother's sons bow down to thee:
cursed be every one that curseth thee, and
blessed be he that blesseth thee.

    The Bible, Genesis 27:28-29

The first fruits of your grain, of your wine and
of your oil, and the first of the fleece of your
sheep, you shall give him.

    The Bible, Deuteronomy 18:4

He who drinks gets drunk;
He who gets drunk goes to sleep;
He who goes to sleep does not sin;
He who does not sin goes to heaven;
So let's all drink and go to Heaven.

    Teri Fortino-Dauenhauer

*And spend the money for whatever you desire,
oxen, or sheep, or wine or strong drink,
whatever your appetite craves; and you shall eat
there before the LORD your God and rejoice,
you and your household.*
The Bible, Deuteronomy 14:26

*And on the day when you wave the sheaf, you
shall offer a male lamb a year old without
blemish as a burnt offering to the LORD. And
the cereal offering with it shall be two tenths of
an ephah of fine flour mixed with oil, to be
offered by fire to the LORD, a pleasing odor;
and the drink offering with it shall be of wine, a
fourth of a hin.*
The Bible, Leviticus 23:12-13

*All the best of the oil, and all the best of the
wine and of the grain, the first fruits of what
they give to the LORD, I give to you.*
The Bible, Numbers 18:12

*To drink wine is to be a good Catholic... To
drink only water, and to have a hatred for wine,
is pure heresy close to atheism.*
Beroalde DeVerville

He will give the rain for your land in its season,
the early rain and the later rain, that you may
gather in your grain and your wine and your oil.
  The Bible, Deuteronomy 11:14

Nothing more excellent nor more valuable than
wine was ever granted mankind by God.
  Plato (427-347 B.C.)

I'm so holy that when I drink wine,
it turns into water.
  Aga Khan III

Bacchus, *n. A convenient deity invented by the*
ancients as an excuse for getting drunk.
  Ambrose Bierce
  from *Enlarged Devil's Dictionary*

Jesus said unto them, 'Fill the waterpots with
water.' And they filled them to the brim.
He said to them, 'Draw out now and bear
to the governor of the feast.' And they bare it...,
the rule of the feast tasted the water that
was made wine.

The Bible, St. John 2:7-9

Chapter IX

Wine Tasting Talk

Few things have been pontificated about more than wine. Wine tasting has its own vocabulary with words that are a foreign language in the tongue spoken. The value of all this critical commentary upon tasting wine is highly suspect, because one person's plum may very well be another person's prune. The attributes given to wine are innumerable and even include anthropomorphic qualities.

Much of the vocabulary of wine tasting stems from a psychological truism that if you have the right word to identify something, you can perceive it. This truism has been developed by wine enthusiasts into an adjectival palate that is a language unto itself. No matter how abstract, many of these descriptive terms allow the taster to objectively communicate distinctions without which it would not be possible to draw at all. So while we cannot account for everyone's taste, we can at least get a more precise understanding of the taster's experience (and hopefully the wine). This is how wine tasting talk can be both silly, but useful at the same time.

Indeed, tasting wine includes more than just tasting with one's mouth. Following the classic rituals of serious tasting will involve all of your senses: **seeing**, **smelling**, **touching**, and **tasting**. You can even add **hearing** as the wine is poured into your glass and when you consider the exciting resonance of two glasses creating a high-pitched duet upon the toasting which should precede the tasting. (If one is lucky enough not to be drinking alone, the clinking of glasses is a tradition whose historical roots were meant to ward off evil spirits.) A capsulation of each part of the ritual is as follows:

Seeing. Different wines have different colors and optical densities. Younger wines tend to be lighter in color, whether white or red. Too much brown is an indication that the wine has prematurely oxidized (air has been allowed into the bottle).

Smelling. Several swirls of your glass will more quickly enable vaporization (volatilization of the esters) of the wine which will release its scents to your nose. While taste is perceived on the tongue, flavor comes from scent.

Touching. This sensation is achieved by letting the wine dance around in your mouth before swallowing it. This allows appreciation of the body (light to full and rich) and the texture (smooth, coarse or sparkling) of the wine.

Tasting. Finally, once the wine is allowed to proceed over the back of the tongue and into the throat, the full style and flavor of a wine can be appreciated. The harmony of the wine's body, texture, flavor, sweetness/ bitterness balance and acidity level creates a dynamic that results in various levels of acceptance and enjoyment.

Some would say there are six distinct stages of wine tasting. These stages have been visually popularized by the noted artist Karen Brussat Butler in a limited edition set of six prints labeled, "See," "Swirl," "Smell," "Sip," "Savor," and "Summarize."

I believe the admonition on tasting and evaluating wine given by Hugh Johnson to wine critics says it all: His wisdom: ... "no critic should forget, as he dallies with epithets, sipping his oak-fermented Chardonnay, or rates one precious bottle half a point behind another, that wine is one of the miracles of nature, and that its 10,000 years of partnership with man has not removed that element of mystery, that independent life that alone among all our foods has made men think of it as divine." (Hugh Johnson, in *Wine*.) Mr. Johnson's admonition is complimented, albeit to every wine drinker, by Derek Cooper who cautions all of us, "As long as we remember the distinctions that ought to be drawn between what we like and what we think we ought to like then we'll preserve our sense of proportion and humour. Wine is there, like food, to be enjoyed; an occasion for relaxation. If we're going to worry about it then we'd be better off putting the corkscrew back in the drawer." (Derek Cooper from *Wine With Food*).

No other beverage makes people want to judge it upon every sip and to then be so eloquent in describing not only what they taste, but also what they imagine they taste. What follows is a very incomplete list of tasting notes used to describe various wines in issues of *Appelation, Wine Enthusiast,* and *Wine Spectator*.

aggressive	brisk	dazzling
angular	brooding	decadent
animated	bubbly	discreet
aristocratic	bumptious	dumb
aromatic	burly	dusky
audacious	cheeky	dynamic
austere	cheerful	earthy
big	chewy	effervescent
blossoming	chic	elegant
bosomy	chirpy	energetic
bouncy	chunky	enthusiastic
bracing	classy	exuberant
brawny	cloying	fizzy

flabby
fleshy
flirty
forceful
friendly
full figure
full of life
gawky
gorgeous
grandiose
gulpable
gutsy
heady
hearty
hefty
high-spirited
indomitable
inky
insolent
lean
lively
lots of
   backbone
lowering
luscious
lush
luxuriant
majestic

masculine
mellow
melodious
murky
muscular
musty
noble
opulent
overblown
pithy
playful
plucky
plummy
plump
puffed up
pulsating
punchy
pungent
racy
refined
regal
restrained
reticent
robust
round
rugged
rustic barnyard
sagging

savory
searingly acidic
seductive
shadowy
silky
skinny
sophisticated
spanking
sparkling
spindly
spirited
spritzy
steely
stringy
succulent
sumptuous
sweaty
syrupy
tangy
toothgripping
vibrant
vigorous
vivacious
voluptuous
zingy
zippy

A cracker, a firecracker, a humdinger
A love-it-or-loathe-it-but-never-fail-
    to-recognize-it kind of wine
Red gut rot; blood-guts-and-thunder
A real mouthfiller; blockbuster fruit
A dinosaur of a red
Mind-numbingly intense
Sheer tooth-rattling-delight

As of yet, no research, or other learning for
that matter, can account for some of your author's
favorite flavor frivolities from "reliable sources."
They are as follows:

Musty rustic funk
Strawberry jam, compost and cabbage
Cat's pee on a gooseberry bush
An iron fist in a velvet glove
"Winy"

The complexity of wine is also a
co-conspirator in these highly inventive word
pursuits. For example, it is neither coincidence nor
imagination that accounts for so many tasting
accolades that attribute a particular fruit taste to a
wine. According to research at the University of
California, Davis and elsewhere, the same chemical
compounds that are found in fruit are also found in

wine. The research reveals, for example, that the reason beaujolais smells of bananas is the common presence of amyl acetate in both bananas and gamay grape.

Wine is like sex in that few men will admit not knowing all about it.
  Hugh Johnson

...to the Royall Oak Tavern ...and here drank a sort of French wine, called Ho Bryan, that hath a good and particular taste that I have never met with.
  Samuel Pepys, *Diary*, April 10, 1663

As to the flavour one might easily go into dythyrambs. Wine-slang talks of the 'finish' in such cases, but this was so full and so complicated that it never seemed to come to a finish. You could mediate on it, and it kept up with your mediations.
  George Saintsbury writing about a red
  Hermitage of 1846 (drunk 40 years later),
  Notes on a Cellar-Book, 1920

...elegant verbal juggling over a glass.
  P. Poupon, *Pensées d'un dégustateur*, 1975

...that nectareous, delicious, precious, heavenly, joyful and divine liquor called wine.
     Rabelais, *Pantagruel*

Within the bottle's depths, the wine's soul sang one night.
     Charles Baudelaire

Okay, so it has sophisticated assertiveness, presumptuous breeding, crisp authority, complex balance, elegant power, and respected fitness. What's it taste like?
     Anonymous

Tell people to trust their own palates, tell people not to be intimidated by the gurus, snobs, and yes, even the wine producer. Tell people if they enjoy a wine, drink it and don't be concerned about whether or not they can articulate why they like it. Wine is like music — you may not know what is good, but you know what you like!
     Justin Meyer

The stomach is the real test-tube for wine.
     Dr. Robert Druitt, *Report on Cheap Wines, Their Use in Diet and Medicine*, 1873

Quality in wines is much easier to recognize than to define.
  Maynard A. Amerine

As a wine drinker but not a wine expert one's tastes are constantly changing.
  Elizabeth David, *An Omelette and a Glass of Wine*

All American wine tastes the same... like Coca Cola.
  Baron Philippe de Rothschild, quoted by Kevin Zraly, *Windows on the World Complete Wine Course*

The great evil of wine is that it first seizes the feet, it is a crafty wrestler.
  Titus Maccius, 190 B.C.

There can be no vocabulary of tasting unless wines have many complex qualities which are worthy of comment... There are millions of bottles of neutral, flabby and impersonal wines about which the taster can say nothing once he has spat them out.
  Emile Peynaud, *The Taste of Wine*, 1983

The whole attraction of wine is that no two bottles are exactly alike, so you have to keep your discrimination ever likely. The standardized article, however good, lulls to sleep this very touchstone of a civilized man.

Edward Bunyard

A young man, invited to a winemen's dinner, invited to give his opinion on one of the wines, held his glass to the light, put it under his nose, surveyed the ceiling with puckered forehead, tasted a little, rolled it once round his mouth, chewed it, consented to swallow, sniffed once more, and finally observed, 'Well, I should call it quite a friendly little wine but – er – scarcely intimate.' Upon which a hard-baked member of the Viticulture Society, sitting alongside asked him, 'Did you really expect it to stand up and embrace you?' Only the word he used was not 'embrace' but something shorter and less delicate!

Walter James

Wine is the first weapon that devils use in attacking the very young.

St. Jerome

Bordeaux: they are neither generous nor vigorous, but the bouquet is not bad, and they have an indescribably sinister, somber bite that is not at all disagreeable.

Attributed to Cardinal Richelieu,
as quoted by Alexandre Dumas

I was convinced forty years ago – and the conviction remains to this day – that in wine tasting and wine talk there is an enormous amount of humbug.

T. G. Shaw

...describe the indescribable.

Emile Peynaud, *The Taste of Wine*, 1983

Burgundy was the winiest wine, the central, essential and typical wine, the soul and greatest common measure of all the kindly wines of the earth.

Charles Edward Montague,
found in *Bartlett's Quotations*

The more specific the name, the better the wine.

Frank Schoonmaker's *Encyclopedia of Wine*

If Claret is the king of natural wines, Burgundy is the queen.
    Moliere

Of the Red wines of Bordeaux the Lafitte is the most choice and delicate, and is characterized by its silky softness on the palate and its charming perfume, which partakes of the violet and the raspberry. The Latour has a fuller body, and at the same time a considerable aroma, but wants the softness of the Lafitte. The Château Margaux is, on the other hand, lighter, and possesses all the delicate qualities of the Lafitte, except that it has not quite so high a flavour. The Haut-Brion, again, has more spirit and body than any of the preceding, but it is rough, when used, and requires to be kept six or seven years in the wood; while the others become fit for bottling in much less time. These are the first-rate wines of the Bordelais.
    Anonymous, *The Wine-Drinker's Manual*, 1830

When it came to writing about wine, I did what almost everybody does − faked it.
    Art Buchwald

There is more rubbish talked about wine and
wine tasting than anything else. It is the perfect
subject for the snob, the bore... and they become
more banal as time goes on.
André Launay

The wine seems to be very closed-in and seems
to have entered a dumb stage. Sort of a Marcel
Meursault.
Paul S. Winalski

It's a naïve domestic Burgundy without any
breeding, but I think you'll be amused
by its presumption.
James Thurber, Caption for Cartoon
in *The New Yorker*

...the bouquet is extraordinary – rich, singed
creosote, cedary, intense, lovely; rich silky,
elegant, long flavour, very dry finish.
Michael Broadbent of a Chateau Margaux 1961

The aristocrat of the table, the nature's
gentleman of the cellar... the deeply
knowledgeable, is rarely, if ever, a snob.
Michael Broadbent

Wine, one sip of this will bathe the drooping spirits in delight beyond the bliss of dreams. Be wise and taste.
John Milton

Chapter X

Wine and Trouble

There is no question in my mind that the phrase "too much of a good thing" was first inspired by a morning hangover from the last evening's wine.

To blame or not to blame (alcohol)? That has been the question since man first fermented. Aristotle stifled the debate when he came down on the side that because consuming alcohol is a voluntary act, drinkers should not be allowed to claim diminished capacity as a defense to criminal conduct. However, in the 13th Century, Thomas Aquinas, the stalwart Catholic theologian, maintained that drunkenness is not a sin and concluded that a drinker should not be held accountable for his actions if he did not know "the strength of the wine."

For years, common law in the United States generally followed the Aquinas principle. Involuntary intoxication was a defense to all crimes, while voluntary intoxication could mitigate the element of specific intent necessary to prove guilt of some crimes, including serious violent crimes such as murder. By the mid-1990s, a few states had passed statutes barring evidence of voluntary intoxication for purposes of determining intent. Bolstered by a 1996 Supreme Court decision, more states adopted statutes barring such evidence, but still only 15 states do. Those states are: Arizona,

Arkansas, Delaware, Florida, Georgia, Hawaii,
Idaho, Michigan, Mississippi, Missouri, Montana,
Pennsylvania, Oklahoma, South Carolina,
and Texas.

*I feel sorry for people who don't drink, because
when they get up in the morning, they're not
going to feel any better all day.*
    Phil Harris

*One may hide all else... but not these two
things... that he is drinking wine, and that he
has fallen in love. Both betray him through his
eyes and through his words, so that the more he
denies, the more they make it plain.*
    Athenaeus of Naucratis,
    The Deipnosophists 2.38.B-C

God made Man
Frail as a bubble,
God made Love,
Love made Trouble
God made the Vine
Was it a sin
That Man made Wine
To drown Trouble in.
    Oliver Herford (1863-1935), A Plea

He talked with more claret than clarity.
    Susan Ertz

The cheapness of wine seems to be a cause, not of drunkenness but of sobriety.... People are seldom guilty of excess in what is their daily fare... On the contrary, in the countries which, either from excessive heat or cold, produce no grapes, and where wine consequently is dear and a rarity, drunkenness is a common vice.
Adam Smith found in *The Wealth of Nations*

Men are like wine − some turn to vinegar, but the best improve with age.
Pope John XXIII

There are no sorrows wine cannot allay,
There are no sins wine cannot wash away,
There are no riddles wine knows not to read,
There are no debts wine is too poor to pay!
Richard Le Gallienne

Wine is only sweet to happy men.
John Keats in a letter to Fanny Brawne, 1819

To give wine to youths is like adding fire to a fire already prepared with matchwood. Young adults should take it in moderation. But elderly persons may take as much as they can tolerate. Wine is borne better in a cold country than in a hot one.
Ibn Sina of Afshena (Avicenna), Canon 809

One barrel of wine can work more miracles than a church full of saints.
    Italian Proverb

Wine cheers the sad, revives the old, inspires the young, makes weariness forget his toil.
    Lord Byron

There is hardly anything that you can't 'walk off', and we walked off this pleasing but perilous predicament.
    George Saintsbury,
    Notes on a Cellar-Book, 1920

When a man eats the fruit of the vine, he is as gentle as a lamb; when he drinks wine he believes himself a lion; if, by chance, he drinks too much he grimaces like a monkey; and when he is often drunk he is nothing more than a vile pig.
    The Talmud

You see, madam, your wine is like the nepenthe of Helen, for it gives the cares as well as the senses of your guests to oblivion.
    Sydney Owenson Morgan

Wine and wenches empty men's purses.
    English Proverb

The chief thing in the art of drinking wine is to keep within those salutary limits which mark the beneficial from the pernicious. In good society, in the present day, this line is well defined; but... the difficulty is to keep the mean in those cases where others have no regard to it. This is best done by studying self-respect, and the art of saying 'no' when the necessity for saying 'no' is strongly felt. The courage to do this, and that absence of all fear of being accounted singular... will prevent suffering in stomach or moral character.

Cyrus Redding, *Every Man His Own Butler*, 1839

There is a devil in every berry of the grape.

The Koran

Give strong drink unto him that is ready to perish, and wine unto those that be of heavy hearts. Let him drink, and forget his poverty, and remember his misery no more.

The Bible, Proverbs 31:6-7

An alcoholic is someone you don't like who drinks as much as you do.

Dylan Thomas (1914-1953)

Wine carries no rudder.

Latin Proverb

I drink one glass for health, a second for refreshment, a third for a friend; but he that offers a fourth is an enemy.
Sir William Temple

Wine gives a man nothing. It neither gives him knowledge nor wit; it only animates a man, and enables him to bring out what a dread of the company has repressed. This is one of the disadvantages of wine: it makes a man mistake words for thoughts.
Samuel Johnson

Wine is a mocker, strong drink is raging, and whosoever is deceived thereby is not wise.
The Bible, Proverbs 20:1

If wine were made accessible to all classes in this country, temperance societies would soon be superfluous. For when the frugal meal of our humble labourer and artisan is cheered (as elsewhere) by a wholesome and invigorating beverage, drunkenness will gradually disappear.
Wine in Relation to Temperance

Who hath woe? Who hath sorrow? Who hath contentions? Who hath battling? Who hath wounds without cause? Who hath redness of eyes? They that tarry long at the wine.
The Bible, Proverbs 23:29-30

If we consult experience, the cheapness of wine seems to be a cause, not of drunkenness, but of sobriety... On the Continent, where wine is cheap, as in France, and where the quantity drunk seems to us quite enormous, ... drunkenness is hardly known.
  Adam Smith

Let us acknowledge the evils of alcohol and strive to eliminate the wine cellar — one glass at a time.
  Anonymous

O God, that men should put an enemy in their mouths to steal away their brains!
  Shakespeare, *Othello*, Act II, Scene 3

One that hath wine as a chain about his wits, such a one lives no life at all.
  Demetrius, *On Poems*

How exceeding strong is wine! It causeth all men to err who drink it.
  Hebrew Scripture, 1 Esdras, III, 18

I am falser than vows made in wine.
  Shakespeare, *As You Like It*, Act III, Line 73

Eat bread of pleasure, drink wine by measure.
  Randal Cosgrove

Songs but solace for a day
Wines a traitor not to trust;
Love's a kiss and then away;
Time's a peddler deals in dust.
> Robert Underwood Johnson (1853-1937),
> "Hearth-Song," Stanza 2

Good wine ruins the purse; bad wine
ruins the stomach.
> Anonymous

Tis pity wine should be so deleterious,
For tea and coffee leave us much more serious.
> Lord George Byron

Woe to those who rise early in the morning, that
they may run after strong drink, who tarry late
into the evening till wine inflames them!
> The Bible, Isaiah 5:11

No more do they drink wine with sinking; strong
drink is bitter to those who drink it. The city of
chaos is broken down, every house is shut up so
that none can enter. There is an outcry in the
streets for lack of wine; all joy has reached its
eventide; the gladness of the earth is banished.
> The Bible, Isaiah 24:9-11

Wine has drowned more men than the sea.
> Latin Proverb

Some people spend the day complaining of a headache, and the night in drinking the wine that gives it.
  Johann Wolfgang von Goethe

A man's palate can become saturated, and after three glasses the best of wines produces only a dull impression.
  Brillat-Savarin, *La Physiologie du goût*

At the first cup man drinks wine, at the second wine drinks wine, at the third wine drinks man.
  Japanese Proverb

Actually, it takes one drink to get me loaded. Trouble is, I can't remember if it's the thirteenth or the fourteenth.
  George Burns

A man is never drunk if he can lie on the floor without holding on.
  Joe E. Lewis

O thou invisible spirit of wine, if thou hast no name to be known by, let us call thee devil!
  William Shakespeare, *Othello*, Act II, Scene 3

Wine is a cunning wrestler; it catches you by the feet.
  Latin Proverb

Wine gives spirit to those who know how to taste it, but it punishes those who drink it without restraint.
    Georges Duhamel

The wine bears three kinds of grapes: the first of pleasure, the next of intoxication, and the third of disgust.
    Anarchis

Chapter XI

Wine and Women

While this section is entitled "Wine and Women," it is when men are added that this association creates the triangular dynamics which have given wine an immortal role in the seducing, loving, marrying, and losing of a woman by a man. History, if not our own experience, tells us that men indiscriminately use wine not only to help lure women, but also as solace for losing them.

Perhaps no other beverage than wine has inspired men more in their relationships with women, even if only in a fanciful way. What man has not opened a bottle of champagne with his love thinking about uncorking more than just bubbles. Despite the uncertainties of relationships between men and women, adding a bubbly accent of champagne to any occasion raises the emotive quality to a definitely more heightened level.

Aristophanes said in 411 B.C. – "Can't live with them, or without them." It is not surprising then that we find many eloquent passages weaving wine into the alternating storm and calm between the sexes. Perhaps if there had been wine in the Garden of Eden, then pursuits dulling curiosity with the apple would have prevailed and that forsaken bite would not have changed everything.

Few things surpass old wine;
and they preach who pleases,
the more because they preach in vain,
Let us have wine and women,
   mirth and laughter,
sermons and soda-water the day after.
   Lord Byron (1788-1824)

Wine prepares the heart for love, unless you
take too much.
   Ovid, *Remediorum Amoris*

Good wine should be taken in sips,
Just like the way I kiss your lips.
   Loh Lik Wei

If a life of wine, women and song get too much,
give up the singing.
   Anonymous

Many a Miss would not be a Missus,
If Liquor did not add spark to her kisses.
   Bill Tennenbaum

There are people who have been known to prefer
bad wine to good, just as there are men who are
fascinated by bad women.
   André Simon

What priest can join two lovers' hands,
But Wine must seal the marriage-bands?
As is celestial wine was thought
Essential to the sacred knot,
And that each bridegroom and his bride
Believ'd they were not firmly ty'd
Till Bacchus with his bleeding tun,
Had finished what the priest begun.
  The Compleat Vintner, 1720

It warms the blood, adds luster to the eyes,
and wine and love have ever been allies.
  Ovid, The Art of Love

A woman should never been seen eating or
drinking, unless it is lobster and Champagne,
the only true feminine and becoming viands.
  Lord Byron

I may not here omit those two main plagues and
common dotages of humankind, wine and
women, which have infatuated and besotted
myriads of people; they go commonly together.
  Robert Burton, Anatomy of Melancholy

Where there is no wine there is no love.
  Euripedes

181

The glances over cocktails
That seemed to be so sweet
Don't seem quite so amorous
Over the Shredded Wheat.
Anonymous

What, when drunk, one sees in other women,
one sees in Garbo sober.
Kenneth Tynan

Wine is shown off by its glass, just as a
woman's beauty is shown off by her dress.
Alexis Lichine

Woman's Quote of the Day: Men are like fine
wine. They all start out like grapes, and it's our
job to stomp on them and keep them in the dark
until they mature into something you'd like to
have dinner with.

Man's Quote of the Day: Women are like fine
wine. They all start out fresh, fruity, and
intoxicating to the mind and then turn
full-bodied with age, until they go all sour
and vinegary and give you a headache.

Wine and women will make men of
understanding to fall away.
Ecclesiasticus XIX

Brisk methinks I am, and fine,
When I drink my capering wine;
Then to love do I incline,
When I do drink my wanton wine;
And I wish all maidens mine,
When I drink my sprightly wine;
Well I sup, and well I dine,
When I drink my frolic wine;
But I languish, lower, and pine,
When I want my fragrant wine.
Robert Herrick, *Anacreontic Verse*

Wine is a little like love. When the right one
comes along, you know it!
Bolla Wines

Bring me flesh and bring me wine,
Bring me pine-logs hither.
John Mason Neal
from "Good King Wenceslas," Stanza 3

Fill ev'ry glass, for wine inspires us
And fires us
With courage, love and joy
Women and wine should life employ.
Is there ought else on earth desirous?
John Gay (1688-1732)

Who does not love wine, women, and song
remains a fool his whole life long.
Johann Heinrich Vos

Wine is made to be drunk as women are
made to be loved; profit by the freshness of
youth or the splendor of maturity; do
not await decrepitude.
Theophile Malvezin

The custom of saluting [i.e., embracing] ladies
by their relatives and friends was introduced, it
is said, by the early Romans, not out of respect
originally, but to find by their breath whether
they had been drinking wine, this being
criminal for women to do, as it sometimes
led to adultery.
Joseph Haydn, Dictionary of Dates

The famous German poet once was asked which
three things he would take to an island. He
stated: "Poetry, a beautiful woman and enough
bottles of the world's finest wines to survive this
dry period!" Then he was asked what he would
leave back first, if it was allowed to take only
two things to the island, and he briefly replied:
"The poetry." Slightly surprised, the man asked
the next question: "And Sir, what would you
leave back if only one was allowed?" Mr. Goethe

thought for a couple of minutes and answered,
"It depends on the vintage!"
Johann Wolfgang Goethe

*Beaujolais Nouveau, unlike Women — is only
really good when it's young.*
Mark Pollman

Wine, madam, is God's next best gift to man.
Ambrose Bierce, *The Devil's Dictionary*, 1907

*O that you would kiss me with the kisses of your
mouth! For your love is better than wine.*
The Bible, Song of Solomon

*The cellars of Scaurus were renowned, as he had
been able to collect three hundred thousand
amphoras of almost every kind of wine
known — as many as 195 different varieties...
Scaurus took greater care of his cellars than of
his reputation, since he consorted with the most
corrupt men in Rome; but he would not tolerate
that anything that might corrupt his wine should
come near his cellar walls. He once nearly
divorced his wife because she had visited the
place at a time when she was indisposed in the
way that women are; which could, according to
him, make his precious wines turn sour.*
Alexandre Dumas,
Le Grand Dictionnaire de cuisine, 1873

*In the order named these are the hardest to
control: wine, women, and song.*
  Franklin P. Adams

*For not only is taste in wine as subjective as
taste in women, but its enjoyment depends more
on circumstances than does that of almost
any other pleasure.*
  Cyril Ray

*And your kisses like the best wine that goes
down smoothly, gliding over lips and teeth.*
  The Bible, Song of Solomon 7:9

*What man can pretend to be a believer in love
who is an abjurer of wine?*
  Richard Brinsley Sheridan

*To drinking together, the safest form of
sex ever invented.*
  Anonymous

*Burgundy I always think of as the woman of
thirty: it has more body than claret, is richer,
more generous, with a finer perfume;
but it is very intoxicating and should be used
with self restraint.*
  Frank Harris, *My Life and Loves*

Ferment the Gamay from my lands in a
large vat. Add the laughter of a girl, the spring
scents of a garden and a good dose of the
spirit of Montmartre.
Traditional Recipe from the Saint-Amour Area

Wine makes old wives wenches.
John Clarke

It provokes the desire, but it takes
away the performance.
William Shakespeare, *Macbeth*, Act II, Scene 3

Like a beauty in her boudoir, Moulin-a-Vent
smiles through its glass at you, immodestly
exhibiting a carnal-coloured tint... Will astonish
you with the firmness of her flesh....
Note from a French Vineyard

Wine comes in at the mouth
And love comes in at the eye;
That's all we shall know for truth
Before we grow old and die.
I lift the glass to my mouth, I look at you,
and sigh.
William Butler Yeats (1865-1939),
Green Helmet and Other Poems

Is not old wine wholesomest, old pippins
toothsomest, old wood burns brightest, old linen
wash whitest? Old soldiers, sweetheart, are
surest, and old lovers are soundest.
   John Webster, *Westward Hoe*, Act II

A Book of Versus underneath the Bough,
A Jug of Wine, a Loaf of Bread – and Thou.
   Edward Fitzgerald
   from *The Rubaiyat of Omar Khayyam*

Chapter XII

Champagne

That Champagne is a wine there can be no doubt, but also there can be no doubt that it is a special wine and indeed it has earned its own place not only in history, but also in this book. There is no question that more than bubbles are released when a Champagne cork is popped. Champagne's mirth and magic is matched only by the misconceptions as to its origin.

All wines, whether still or sparkling, are the result of the fermentation when yeast cells convert sugar into alcohol and carbonic gas. Making the bubbles in Champagne or sparkling wine, involves adding a separate fermentation process which is conducted in a sealed container to ensure that the carbonic gas does not escape. Carbonic gas remains dissolved in the wine until the cork is removed. The uncorking produces an effervescence. The effervescence of the sparkling wine is called its mousse. There are two basic attributes of this effervescence or mousse. The first its strength or pressure and the second is the size of the bubbles.

The French would have us believe that Dom Perignon invented Champagne, but, while he can be credited with inventing the class Champagne blend from that geographical region of France, the English invented Champagne nearly a decade before Dom Perignon arrived in the Champagne region. Even the very first mention of sparkling

Champagne in any language is in English, not French. In 1676, Sir George Etherege wrote this passage in his work, "The Man of Mode:"

To the Mall and the Park
Where we love till 'tis dark, then sparkling
Champaign
Puts an end of their reign;
* It quickly recovers*
* Poor languishing lovers*
Makes us frolic and gay, and drowns all sorrow;
but, Alas, we relapse again on the morrow.

Often called the Inventor of Champagne, Dom Pérignon, while not the inventor, certainly could be accurately called the Dean of Champagne. He insisted on quality-focused vineyard practices; he was the first to limit crop sizes to intensify fruit flavors, and was known to reject even the single grape that was broken or bruised. To this day, his namesake Dom Pérignon Champagne is still considered the benchmark for quality.

It has been the bubbles that have elevated Champagne and sparkling wine to their preeminence as wines of celebration. These sparkling wines have been the defining beverage of celebration at births, christenings, weddings, a new job and retirement. When it comes to launching ships and congratulating automobile racing

winners, the pouring of wine on the ship and the
driver is on an equal, if not greater footing
than drinking it.

These escaping bubbles have the ability to
raise one's spirit, reaffirm one's optimism for life,
to create, sustain, renew and enrich friendships.
Unlike regular wines, neither time nor type
of meal, seems to place any restrictions on its use.
Who ever heard of having wine at breakfast, yet
a Champagne breakfast or brunch is touted as an
upscale pairing. People who would not drink
anything alcoholic at lunch will nevertheless drink
Champagne at lunch with neither guilt nor
admission. Champagne and sparkling wines were
the first wines to have a glass designed for their
particular use. The Champagne flute is not only
functional, but can also be said to have an
elegance well suited for its contents.

Technically, only sparkling wines from the
Champagne region in France can be called
Champagne. In a real but no doubt unsuccessful
attempt to get the world to understand and clear
up this misconception, the popular cult movie
"Wayne's World" contains this instructive dialogue:
Cassandra: "I don't believe I've ever had French
Champagne before." Benjamin Kane: "Oh, actually
all Champagne is French, it's named after the
region. Otherwise it's sparkling white wine.

Americans of course don't recognize the convention so it becomes that thing of calling all of their sparkling white Champagne, even though by definition they're not."

The mere fact that a wine is carbonated, whether white or red, does not make it Champagne, but only "sparkling" wine from wherever it was produced.

I want Champagne to celebrate victory and I need it in defeat.
Winston Churchill

*That winter two things happened which made
me see that the world, the flesh, and the devil
were going to be more powerful influences in
my life after all than the chapel bell. First, I
tasted Champagne; second, the theater.*
    Belle Livingstone

*Can you imagine opening a bottle of champagne
with a bottle opener. I can't. It would eliminate
half the fun.*
    Alain De Vogue, French Vintner

Champagne, the great civilizer.
        Attributed to Talleyrand in *Bottled Wisdom*,
        compiled and edited by Mark Pollman

*There are only two occasions when I drink
Champagne, and these are: when I have game
for dinner and when I haven't.*
    Attributed to S.D. Churchill

*Our champagne is not just about making money.
It is about bringing joy to people.*
    Priest in a small village in Champagne

*Too much of anything is bad, but too much
Champagne is just right.*
    Mark Twain

*To give champagne fair play it ought to be
produced at the very beginning of dinner or at
any rate after one glass of sherry or Madeira.
Any other wines rather unfit the palate for it.*
Thomas Walker, *The Art of Dining*, 1881

*Meeting Roosevelt was like uncorking your first
bottle of Champagne.*
Winston Churchill

*Gentlemen, in the little moment that remains to
us between the crisis and the catastrophe, we
may as well drink a glass of champagne.*
Paul Claudel

*I was enjoying myself now. I had taken two
fingerbowls of Champagne and the scene had
changed before my eyes into something
significant, elemental, and profound.*
F. Scott Fitzgerald

*You can have too much champagne to drink,
but you can never have enough.*
Elmer Rice

Even for those who dislike Champagne...
there are two Champagnes one can't refuse:
Dom Pérignon and the even more superior
Cristal... a chilled fire of such prickly dryness
that, swallowed, seems not to have been
swallowed at all...
  Truman Capote, *Answered Prayers*

I only drink Champagne when I'm happy, and
when I'm sad. Sometimes I drink it when I'm
alone. When I have company, I consider it
obligatory. I trifle with it if I am not hungry and
drink it when I am. Otherwise I never touch it –
unless I'm thirsty.
  Lily Bollinger

Before I was born my mother was in great
agony of spirit and in a tragic situation. She
could take no food except iced oysters and
champagne. If people ask me when I began to
dance, I reply 'In my mother's womb, probably
as a result of the oysters and champagne –
the food of Aphrodite.'
  Isadora Duncan

My only regret in life is that I did not
drink more Champagne.
  John Maynard Keynes (1883-1946)

*The feeling of friendship is like being
comfortably filled with roast beef: Love is like
being enlivened with Champagne.*
     Samuel Johnson

*The sound of thy explosive cork, Champagne,
has, by some strange witchery, all of a sudden
taught men the sweet music of speech.
A murmur as of a rising storm runs round the
table: badinage commences, flirtations
flourish... We might tell of breakfasts, and of
suppers, suddenly converted from Saharas of
intolerable dullness into oases of smiles and
laughter by the appearance of Champagne.*
     Charles Tovey from
     Wit, Wisdom, and Morals, Distilled from Bacchus

*It had the taste of an apple peeled with
a steel knife.*
     Aldous Huxley, Sebastian Barnack,
     in Time Must Have a Stop, assessing a
     Roederer 1916 Champagne

*In victory you deserve Champagne, in defeat,
you need it.*
     Napoleon Bonaparte

There was a young lady from Kent
Who said she knew what men meant
When they asked her to dine
Private room, champagne, wine
She knew what they meant and she went.
  Anonymous

Burgundy for kings, champagne for duchesses,
claret for gentlemen.
  Anon French Proverb

Two warm bodies and one cold bottle of
Champagne will produce something more
wonderful than would happen without the
Champagne.
  Helen Gurley Brown

It has been said that the final sound from the
uncorking of a bottle of Champagne is like the
sigh of a contented woman.
  Douglas Lamb

Champagne is the only wine to leave a woman
beautiful after drinking.
  Madame de Pompadour

How is champagne made? By sheer genius,
sir, sheer genius!
> Conversation at White's Club, London

I like Champagne because it always tastes as
though my foot's asleep.
> Art Buchwald

Come, I am tasting the stars.
> Attributed by legend to
> Dom Pierre Pérignon (1638-1714)

Champagne makes you feel like it's Sunday and
better days are just around the corner.
> Marlene Dietrich

More than any other wine, Champagne is a
luxury brand made and sold by a hard-headed,
hard-working, rather cold-blooded bunch of
people, fully aware that no one needs to drink
Champagne, that its glorious patina needs
constant polishing.
> Nicholas Faith, found in
> The Story of Champagne

Only those who lack in imagination, cannot find
a good reason to drink Champagne.
> Oscar Wilde

Because the King had at one time suffered from severe attacks of gout..., instead of the champagne he had been used to drinking, they had in more recent times made him drink watered-down Burgundy, so old that it had lost its strength... Never did he drink his wine unwatered... So much water, so much fruit, unrelieved by any alcohol, lowered his vital spirits and turned his blood gangrenous.
    Saint-Simon, *Letters*

Three be the things I shall never attain: Envy, content, and sufficient champagne.
    Dorothy Parker

Burgundy makes you think of silly things; Bordeaux makes you talk about them, and Champagne makes you do them.
    Brillat-Savarin

A good party is where you enjoy good people, and they taste even better with Champagne.
    Wilson Mizner

Champagne offers a minimum of alcohol and a maximum of companionship.
    David Niven

Here's to Champagne, the drink divine, that makes us forget all our troubles; It's made of a dollar's worth of wine, and three dollars worth of bubbles.

Anonymous

Chapter XIII

General Extolments

There seems to be no end to the praise of wine. Like a great wonder of nature, men and women have opined of wine's wonderment, no doubt from the time after the first fermentation of the grape. Wine is a living thing, depending upon both the luck of mother nature and the skill of the wine-maker. When the two are in harmony, then it becomes clear what the fuss is all about. This section sets forth an array of extolments on the pleasures of wine which given their breadth and imagination are not capable of any other categorization.

Decanter, *n. A vessel whose functions are most envied by the human stomach.*
    Ambrose Bierce, *The Devil's Dictionary*

The most glorious nectar ever made.
    Jaques Pepin

You Americans have the loveliest wines in the world, you know, but you don't realize it. You call them domestic and that's enough to start trouble anywhere.
    H.G. Wells

The First Duty of wine is to be Red... the second is to be a Burgundy.
    Harry Waugh

Fill every beaker up, my men,
pour forth the cheering wine:
There's life and strength in every drop,
thanksgiving to the vine.

Albert Gorton Greene
from *The Baron's Last Banquet*

O thou the drink of gods, and angels! Wine!

Robert Herrick, *Hesperides*, 1648

I drank at every vine.
The last was like the first.
I came upon no wine.
So wonderful as thirst.

Edna St. Vincent Millay,
Feast, The Harp-Weaver, (1923)

Foolish boy! Why tremblest thou?
Thou lovest it, then, my wine?
Wouldst more of it? See, how glows,
Through the delicate, flush'd marble,
The red, creaming liquor,
Strown with dark seeds!
Drink, thee! I chide thee not,
Deny thee not my bowl.
Come, stretch forth thy hand, thee-so!
Drink-drink again!

Mathew Arnold (1822-1888),
Circe in *The Strayed Reveller*, 1849

Why is there so much wine left at the end of my money?
Milan Maximovich,
Winemaker of Thunder Mountain

There can be no bargain without wine.
Latin Saying

And finally, we can say that alcohol has existed longer than all human memory. It has outlived generations, nations, epochs and ages. It is a part of us, and that is fortunate, indeed. For although alcohol will ways be the master of some, for most of us it will continue to be the servant of man.
Morris E. Chafetz

A bottle of good wine, like a good act, shines ever in the retrospect.
Robert Louis Stevenson

The discovery of a wine is of greater moment than the discovery of a constellation. The universe is too full of stars.
Brillat-Savarin

Bury me beneath a vine And let me pour my soul in thine.
Ralph Steadman

Here's what I like to say about a well made
wine of modest proportions: It is not a wine
that commands your attention, but rather,
rewards it.
Dave Guimond

... Mr. Tulkinghorn sits at one of the open
windows, enjoying a bottle of old port. Though
a hard-grained man, close, dry, and silent, he
can enjoy old wine with the best. He has a
priceless bin of port in some artful cellar under
the Fields, which is one of his many secrets.
When he dines alone in chambers, as he has
dined today, and has his bit of fish and his steak
or chicken brought in from the coffee-house, he
descends with a candle to the echoing regions
below the deserted mansion, and, heralded by
the remote reverberation of thundering doors,
comes gravely back, encircled by an earthy
atmosphere and carrying a bottle from which he
pours a radiant nectar, two score and ten years
old, that blushes in the glass to find itself so
famous, and fills the whole room with the
fragrance of southern grapes.
Charles Dickens, Bleak House

No one that has drunk old wine wants new;
for he says, 'The old is nice.'
The Bible, Luke 5:39

208

...the best utilization of solar energy that we have found... Wine really is bottled sunshine.
Emile Peynaud, *The Taste of Wine*, 1983

Wine improves with age. The older I get, the better I like it.
Anonymous

Watch out when the auctioneer calls some 19th century wine 'a graceful old lady whose wrinkles are starting to show through layers of make-up.' That means the wine is undrinkable, and some fool will spend $500 for it.
Robert Parker

O for a draught of vintage, that hath been cool'd a long age in the deep delved earth.
Keats

A bunch of grapes is beautiful, static and innocent; it is merely fruit. But when it is crushed it becomes an animal, for the crushed grapes become wine and wine has an animal life. Wine suffers a heaving birth. It has a rough, groping childhood. It develops into adolescence. Then, if it does not sicken, it matures; and in this it is almost human since it does not mature according to the laws of its particular and individual personality.
William Younger

209

Behold, my heart is like wine that has no vent;
like new wineskins, it is ready to burst.
The Bible, Job 32:19

As far as I am concerned there are only two
types of wine, those I like and those I don't.
André Launay

There is simply nothing else that so perfectly
encapsulates physical sensation, social
well-being and aesthetic exploration at
the same time.
Hugh Johnson from *Hugh Johnson's Pocket Wine Book*

Good wine praises itself.
Dutch Proverb

Chapter XIV

Glossary
of
Sources
for Quoted Material

Adams, Franklin P.: Poet, born in 1881. He wrote such poems as "To Alice-Sit-By-The Hour," "Prohibition" and "Baseball's Sad Lexicon." He is responsible for such quotes as, "ninety-two percent of the stuff told you in confidence you couldn't get anyone else to listen to."

Addison, Joseph (1672-1719): English essayist, poet, statesman, and translator of Virgil's Georgics. He was educated at Charterhouse and at Oxford, where he became a distinguished classical scholar. His works also include an opera libretto, *Rosamund*; a prose comedy, *The Drummer*; and a neoclassical tragedy, *Cato*.

Aeschylus (525-456 B.C.): Athenian tragic dramatist, known as the "Father of Tragedy." He wrote between 80 and 90 plays. Seven tragedies survive intact, along with fragments of other works. He is thought to have written his first plays around the year 500, for the legendary dramatic competition, the Great Dionysa, at the Festival of Dionysus in Athens, where they were performed. He won 13 victories at the Great Dionysia.

Alciatore, Roy Louis (1902-1972): Businessman, he managed a well-known restaurant, Antoine's, in New Orleans for over 40 years, during the turbulent Prohibition and World War II era.

Aldrich, T.B. (1836-1907): Writer and poet. He was born in Portsmouth, New Hampshire. He was a publisher until moving to Boston in 1865. In 1881, he became a writer for the *Atlantic Monthly*. Aldrich remains best-known for his book, *The Story of a Bad Boy*, but he is also well-known for the publication of many of his poems in various journals.

Al-Khayyam, Omar: Middle Ages mathematician and astronomer. He was also well known as a poet, philosopher, and physician. He is perhaps best known for his poetic work *Rubaiyat*, which was translated by Edward Fitzgerald in 1859.

Allen, H. Warner: Author, writer and poet. He wrote *A Contemplation of Wine* in 1950.

Allen, Hervey: Born in Pittsburgh, 1889, he published his first work (a book of poetry), entitled *On the Border* in 1916. He fought and was wounded in World War I. His wartime experience gave him the inspiration for another book, *Toward the Flame* (1926). In 1933, he published *Anthony Adverse*, a widely acclaimed book set in Europe during the Napoleonic era. He died in 1949 while working on the fourth book of his planned five-book series about colonial America.

Amerine, Maynard A.: Contemporary writer. He wrote: *A Bibliography on Grapes, Wines,*

Other Alcoholic Beverages, and Temperance; Wine: an
Introduction; Wine; Wine and Must Analysis; Checklist of
Books and Pamphlets on Grapes and Wines and
Other Related Subjects 1938-1948.

Anacreon: Greek poet who was born in 570
B.C, and wrote poems about wine and love.

Anderson, Burton: Contemporary writer and
well-known authority on Italian wine. He has lived
in Tuscany for over 25 years, and is the former
editor of the *International Herald Tribune* in Paris. He
has won several major wine awards in Italy, and has
also been honored by wine publications in the U.S.
and Britain. He has written such books as *Vino,*
Wines of Italy, Treasures of the Italian Table and *The Wine*
Atlas of Italy.

Andrieu, Pierre (1821-1892): French painter.
His paintings are displayed in such museums as
National Gallery in London, England and the Musée
des Augustins in Tolouse, France.

Anonymous : Although often
quoted in this book, nothing is
known about Anonymous except for
the fact that he or she seems to have
an appreciation of wine and a
well-turned phrase.

Aquinas, Saint Thomas: Philosopher, born in 1225 in Italy. One of the greatest philosophers in the history of the Catholic Church. He joined the Dominican order and became a priest in 1250. He started teaching at the University of Paris in 1252. He served as an advisor in the papal court from 1259 to 1268. Among his work are *Summa Contra Gentiles* (on the truth of the Catholic faith) and *Summa Theologica* (Summary Treatise of Theology). He was canonized by Pope John XXII in 1323 and proclaimed a Doctor of the Church by Pope Pius V in 1567.

Aristophenes (Born around 456 B.C.-380 B.C.): Comic poet in ancient Athens, known for writing satire critical of politicians and even philosophers such as Socrates.

Arnold, Mathew: Poet. Born in England in 1822. He was the professor of poetry at Oxford from 1857 to 1867, where he was the first professor to lecture in English, rather than Latin. Among his works are *Poems, On Translating Homer,* and *Essays in Criticism.* Later in life his focus changed from criticisms on poetry to religious and social criticism, and he published such works as *Culture and Anarchy, Friendship's Garland,* and *Literature and Dogma.*

Asher, Gerald: Contemporary journalist. He is currently the wine editor for *Gourmet* magazine.

Athenaeus of Naucratis: Writer. He lived in the Roman Empire at the civilization's peak and was the author of *Deipnosophistae*, a collection of after-dinner stories.

Austen, Jane: Writer. Born in England in 1775. She is regarded as one of the greatest writers in the history of English literature. Her works include the novels *Pride and Prejudice, Sense and Sensibility, Mansfield Park*, and *Emma*.

Bacon, Sir Francis: Lawyer, statesman, philosopher, and master of the English language, born in 1561. His sharp worldly wisdom is displayed in his famous essays. He was acclaimed for his power as a speaker in Parliament, and his legal prowess was displayed in famous trials and as James I's Lord Chancellor.

Barkley, Alben W.: Politician. Born in Kentucky in 1877. He graduated from law school and was admitted to the Kentucky bar in 1901, where he was a prosecutor and then judge. He served in the House of Representatives from 1912 to 1927, and in the Senate from 1927-1948. While in Congress he helped Franklin Roosevelt design and pass the New Deal legislation. He served as Vice-President under Harry S. Truman from 1948 to 1952.

Barther, Edouard: A French government deputy and wine lobbyist who called for wine canteens to be established at every railroad station where soldiers would gather during World War II.

Barthes, Roland: Contemporary writer. Born in France. He is one of the most important international, intellectual figures to have emerged in postwar France and his writings continue to have an influence on critical debates today.

Baudelaire, Charles: Poet, writer. Born in Paris, France in 1821.

Bell, Madison Smart: Contemporary writer. He is the author of nine novels, including *The Washington Square Ensemble, Waiting for the End of the World, Straight Cut, The Year of Silence, Doctor Sleep, Save Me, Joe Louis,* and *Soldier's Joy.*

Benwell, William Samuel: He wrote *Simpson's Contemporary Quotations*, a book concerning the dealings of society, including communication, the fine arts, and food and drink.

Bernstein, Leonard: Musician and composer. Born in Lawrence, Massachusetts in 1918. He graduated from Harvard in 1939, and by 1958 he had become the Music Director of the New York Philharmonic. He is perhaps best known for writing the musicals *West Side Story* and *Candide*.

Berry, Charles Walter: Businessman and writer. Born in England. He was a member of the Berry family, which has owned and operated Berry Bros. Wine in London for over 300 years. In 1933 he published *In Search of Wine*.

Bertall, Louis: Writer. He wrote *La Vigne: Voyage autour des Vins de France*, which was published in Paris, France in 1877.

Bespaloff, Alex: Contemporary writer. He is the writer of *New Frank Schoonmaker's Encyclopedia of Wine*, a comprehensive wine encyclopedia including the names of several thousand wines, a pronunciation guide of foreign wine names, and a list of French wines. He is also the author of *Alexis Bespaloff's Complete Guide to Wine*, and *The New Signet Book of Wine*.

Betjeman, John: Poet and journalist. Born in London in 1906. During World War II he was the press attaché to the minister of Ireland, and he also worked in the ministry of information. He became known as one of Great Britain's most popular poets. Among his works are *Mt. Zion, Continental Dew,* and *High and Low.*

Bierce, Ambrose: Writer and journalist. Born in Ohio in 1842. He fought for the Union Army during the Civil War, and was wounded in the Battle of Kenesaw Mountain. After the war he moved to San Francisco and became a journalist. From 1887 to 1896 he wrote a column for William Randolph Hurst's The *San Fransico Examiner* called the *Prattler Column.* In 1892 he wrote the book *In the Midst of Life.* He moved to Washington D.C. in 1896, where he wrote for *The American.* In 1913 he became disillusioned with life in America and moved to Mexico, where he disappeared. He was believed to have been caught up in Pancho Villa's revolution. Among his other works are *Can Such Things Be* and *The Devil's Dictionary.*

Blackie, John Stuart: Scottish poet. Born in Aberdeen in 1809. After receiving a law degree from the University of Edinburgh, he became a professor of humanity at Marischal College in Aberdeen. In 1860, he became the chair of Greek at the University of Edinburgh.

 **Bonaparte, Napoleon**: Born in France in 1769. He received his commission to the artillery in 1785, and became a General in 1793. In 1796 he achieved the rank of Commander in Chief of the Army of Italy. He achieved notoriety with a series of military victories from 1796-1799. In 1804 he had himself declared Emperor of France. He achieved a succession of military victories, and soon most of Europe was under his control. His unsuccessful invasion of Russia in 1812 was the beginning of the end, which occurred at Waterloo in 1815. After this defeat, he spent the rest of his life as a prisoner of war on the island of Saint Helena.

Boorde, Andrew: Middle Ages English physician who spent his life traveling and writing about what he observed in different regions. His commentary often delved into the drinking habits of the local population of most of the countries in Europe. His guidebook *First Book of the Introduction of Knowledge* was published in 1548. He also wrote *Dietary of Health* in 1542.

Boswell, James (1740-1795): Writer. Born in Edinburgh, and educated at the universities of Glasgow, Edinburgh, and Utrecht. He was admitted to both the Scottish and English bars and practiced law but primarily pursued a literary career. In 1773, he was admitted to Johnson's Literary Club, which included statesman Edmund Burke, writer Oliver Goldsmith, and painter Sir Joshua Reynolds. He is best known for writing the biography *The Life of Samuel Johnson, L.L.D.*

Boulestin, X.M.: Contemporary chef and writer. He owned his own restaurant, Boulestin's, which served French Cuisine. In 1937 he became the first chef to appear on British Television. In 1975 he wrote *Boulstein's Round-the Year Cookbook*.

Brillat-Savarin, Jean Anthelme (1755-1826): French lawyer and politician who achieved fame through a book, *Physiologie du Gout*. This work on gastronomy has been described as the "finest book of its kind in the Western world." Numerous translations have appeared in English under such titles as *Gastronomy as a Fine Art*, *The Science of Good Living*, *The Handbook of Dining*, and *The Physiology of Taste or Meditations on Transcendental Gastronomy*.

Brinton, Dr. William: Contemporary agron-
omist and writer. He is the director of the Wood's
End Agricultural Institute in Mt. Vernon, Maine. He
is an expert on composting, and has written many
articles on the subject.

Broadbent, Michael: Chairman of Christie's
International Wine Department, former Chairman
of The Institute of Masters of Wine and immediate
Past-President of The International Wine and
Food Society. He is the author of *Wine Vintages*
and *Winetasting*.

Brown, Greg: Contemporary businessman. He
is founder of T-Vine. "T" in T-Vine stands for
Trinity, which represents body, mind and spirit. His
first label read, "I like wines the way I like family
and friends. Obnoxiously forward."

Brown, Helen Gurley: Writer. Born in 1922
in Green Forest, Arkansas. She wrote the best seller
Sex and the Single Girl in 1962, and then became the
editor in chief of *Cosmopolitan* magazine in 1965. In
1996 she received the American Society of
Magazine Editors Hall of Fame Award.

Buchwald, Art: Contemporary writer. This newspaper columnist won the Pulitzer Prize for Distinguished Commentary in 1982. He has written 30 books, including the best-selling *I Think I Don't Remember.*

Buckley, William F.: Contemporary journalist. One of the most versatile public figures in America, he is the authoritative journalistic voice of conservatism today. He is founder of *National Review*, the journal of conservative thought and opinion. Author of many best-selling books, including *God and Man at Yale*, *Saving the Queen*, *Stained Glass* and *Overdrive*.

Buning, Werumeus: Dutch poet, born in 1891.

Bunyard, Edward: Contemporary writer. Wrote the book *The Anatomy of Dessert*. He was especially fond of apples and pears. He wrote that with apples, "the *crunch* is the thing, a certain joy in crashing through living tissue, a memory of Neanderthal days."

Burns, George: Actor. Born in Manhattan in 1896. He began his long career in show business singing and dancing in vaudeville shows. He married actress Gracie Allen in 1926. In 1976 he won an Oscar for Best Supporting Actor. Known for his wit and trademark cigar. He died in 1996, not long after turning 100 years old. He once said, "Fall in love with what you do for a living. I don't care what it is. It works."

Burton, Robert: Writer. Born in England in 1577. He spent his entire life as the librarian at Christ Church, Oxford. He is best known for writing *The Anatomy of Melancholy*.

Busby, James (1802-1871): Viticulturalist, British resident, farmer, politician, newspaper editor, he was known as "the father of Australian viticulture."

Byron, Lord George: English poet. Born in London in 1788. His works include *Don Juan* and *Childe Harold's Pilgrimage*. In 1824 he went to Greece to fight for Greek Independence, where he died.

Capote, Truman: Writer. Born in New Orleans in 1924. He wrote such novels as *Other Voices, Other Rooms*, *Breakfast at Tiffany's* and the highly acclaimed non-fiction *In Cold Blood* about the murder of a Kansas family by two young drifters.

Carroll, Lewis: Writer and inventor. Best known for writing *Alice's Adventures in Wonderland* and *Through the Looking-Glass*. He was also known for his many inventions.

Chafetz, Morris E.: Contemporary writer. He wrote *Alcoholism and Society,[1962]*; *Liquor: the servant of man,[1965]*; *Why drinking can be good for you, [1976]*. Editor of *Frontiers of alcoholism, [1970]*. He is a leading expert in the field of alcoholism.

Child, Julia: Writer and chef. Born in Pasadena, California, and graduated from Smith College in 1934. During World War II she served with the Office of Strategic Services in Washington DC, Ceylon (now Sri Lanka), and China. After the war, her husband, Paul Child, was assigned to the U.S. Information Service at the American Embassy in Paris. In Paris, she started her culinary career at the Cordon Bleu. In collaboration with her two French colleagues, Simone Beck and Louisette Bertholle, she wrote *Mastering the Art of French Cooking*, which appeared in 1961. The book gave birth to the PBS television series *The French Chef* and was followed by several other series including her *Master Chef* programs, in which she was host to 26 of America's well-known chefs.

St. Chrysostom: Cleric and writer. Born in Antioch in 347 AD, he became a priest in 386 and patriarch of Constantinople in 398. His writings and speeches were very influential in his day. He was banished from Constantinople for criticizing the Roman Emperor of the East. He wrote a popular treatise on the priesthood in 381. He was declared the patron of preachers in 1909 by Pope Pius X.

Churchill, Winston (1874-1965): Politician. He became a military correspondent and won many accolades for his coverage of various stories in India and in South Africa during the second Boer War. He was Great Britain's Secretary of the Navy during World War I. He became Prime Minister in 1940, and led his country through World War II. He was knighted in 1953, and also received the Nobel Peace Prize for his writings covering World War II.

Clarke, John: Politician. Born in England in 1609. In 1638 he founded the first Baptist Church in America. He later served in the Rhode Island General Assembly, and also as the Deputy Governor of Rhode Island.

Clarke, Marcus (1846-1881): Writer and librarian. His first novel, *Long Odds*, appeared in 1868-69.

Clarke, Oz: One of the world's leading wine experts. He has won all the major wine writing awards both in the UK and the USA. He is the author of numerous best-selling books.

Claudel, Paul: Author. Born in 1868. A writer of his time, the Bible became his inspiration. He was a diplomat to several European and Eastern countries.

Clement of Alexandria: Early Christian thinker and writer of the late second century and early third century AD.

Cogan, Thomas: Elizabethan dietitian. He was the author of *The Haven of Health*.

Colette, Sidonie-Gabrielle: Writer. Born in France in 1873.

Conklin, Thomas: Contemporary writer. Wrote such books as *Muhammad Ali*, *Adventures of Hercules* and *Titanic Sinks*.

Constantin-Weyer, M.: French writer. Born in 1881. In 1928 he wrote the book *Un homme se penche sur son passé* and became the editor of *Le Journal de l'Ouest*.

Cooper, Alfred Duff: British politician. He was elected to Parliament in 1924. He served as Secretary of War from 1935 to 1937; as Minister of Information from 1940-1941; and was ambassador to France from 1944-1947. He wrote the book *Old Men Forget* in 1953.

Cooper, Derek: Contemporary writer. He has presented BBC Radio 4's *The Food Programme* since 1979. He has written 18 books and regularly writes for magazines and papers on food issues.

Crabbe, George (1754-1832): English poet. In 1783 he wrote his most famous work, *The Village*. He also wrote *The Library, The Parrish Register, The Borough,* and *Tales.*

David, Elizabeth: Writer. Author of: *An Omelette And A Glass; Elizabeth David Classics; English Bread And Yeast; French Country Cooking; French Provincial Cooking; Italian Food;* and *Summer Cooking.*

Davies, W.H. (1871-1940): Writer. Born in Newport, Monmouthshire. His first attempt at poetry, *The Soul's Destroyer*, printed at his own expense, won the favorable attention of George Bernard Shaw. Thereafter, his success was assured. Next, *The Autobiography of a Super-Tramp* describes his vagabond life. He was a prolific poet, his favorite themes were nature and the hardships of the poor.

Demetrius: Soldier and leader, who ruled over Macedonia and died in 283 B.C.

DeVerville, Beroalde: French writer and artist who lived from 1556 to about 1629.

Dickens, Charles (1812-1870): Born in England. He is known as the author of *Child's History of England, Hard Times, A Tale of Two Cities, Great Expectations, A Christmas Carol,* and *Oliver Twist.* He is one of the best known and most popular British novelists.

Dietrich, Marlene: Singer and actress. She was born in 1901. She started to work in film with director Steinberg, who transformed her into a star, the vision of his perfect woman. Even though she had been born in Germany, Dietrich opposed the Third Reich and became a U.S. citizen at the outbreak of World War II.

Dineson, Isak: Writer. Born in Denmark in 1885. Her real name was Karen Blixen, but she wrote under the pen name of Isak Dineson. She was married in 1914 and moved to Kenya, where she lived on a coffee plantation. She divorced in 1921, and moved back to Denmark. She is perhaps best known for writing *Out of Africa*.

Diogenes: Greek philosopher, generally considered the founder of the Cynics school of philosophy. Born in Sinope, he studied in Athens. He plunged into a life of austerity, wearing coarse clothing, eating plain food, and sleeping on the bare ground in the open streets or under porticoes.

Dowson, Ernest: Poet. Although he was famous for his religious poetry, he led a life full of alcoholism and debt. He died at age 32 of tuberculosis .

Druitt, Dr. Robert: Physician. He advocates of the use of wines in a regular diet.

Duhamel, Georges: A member of the Academie Francaise and a noted food and wine author.

Duijker, Hubrecht: Contemporary writer. He is one of the world's favorite wine writers. Co-author, with Hugh Johnson, of *The Wine Atlas of France*. He was named Chevalier de l'Ordre du Merite Agricole by the French Government and won the coveted Literary Award of the Bordeaux Academy.

Dumas, Alexandre: Born in 1802 in France. He wrote many interesting anecdotes in *Mes Mémoires*. He is best remembered for his historical novels such as *Monte Cristo*.

Duncan, Isadora: Dancer. Founder of modern dance and a developer of the "natural technique," she sought to distance herself from the still postures and straight lines of ballet.

Duncan, Leslie: Leslie and Peter Duncan helped create a web page on THE BEEFSTEAK AND BURGUNDY CLUB OF SUDBURY, ONTARIO, CANADA. This site has information on various types of wine.

Dunne, Finley Peter: American author. Born in 1867. He wrote a popular column called Mr. Dooley, and was a friend of Mark Twain.

Edward VII (1841–1910): Became the Prince of Wales. As a youth he traveled widely on the Continent and visited the United States, Canada, and the Middle East. A liberal patron of the arts and sciences, he became a leader of fashionable society and an enthusiastic sportsman. He succeeded to the throne on Jan. 22, 1901, at the age of 59 and was crowned on Aug. 9, 1902.

Elkort, Martin: Contemporary author. This author has written such books as *The Secret Life of Food* and *A Feast of Food*.

Emerson, Ralph Waldo: Writer. Attended Harvard from 1817-1821. Served as a pastor of the Old North Church in Boston from 1829 to 1832. Wrote many influential poems on transcendentalism. Delivered a series of famous lectures in the early 1840s, which were collected in his *Essays*.

Ertz, Susan: Contemporary writer.

Euripides: Greek tragedian. Wrote a total of 92 plays. Eighteen of his plays survive.

Fabricant, Florence: Contemporary chef. Wrote the book *Pleasures of the Table*, and also writes a column about food for the *New York Times*.

Fadiman, Clifton (1904-1999): American editor, anthologist, and writer. After graduating from Columbia University, New York City, in 1925, he taught school and then became an editor in the publishing firm of Simon & Schuster. He later became book editor of *The New Yorker* magazine from 1933 to 1943.

Fairbairn, Ann (1901-1972): Author, she wrote the book *Five Smooth Stones* which was published in 1966.

Faith, Nicholas: Contemporary journalist and author, known for writing investigative books, in particular, *Crash and Mayday, Blaze, The Forensics of Fire*, and *Black Box*.

Fiduccia, Peter: Well-known hunter who wrote the book *101 Deer Hunting Tips*. He is also the Editor in Chief of *Outdoorsman's Edge Book Club*.

Fields, W.C.: American comedian. He was a master mimic and actor.

Fitzgerald, Edward: Writer. Born in England in 1809. He is best-known for translating *The Rubaiyat of Omar Khayyam*, a poem by an 11th or 12th century Persian poet, into English.

Fitzgerald, F. Scott: Writer. Born in St. Paul, Minnesota in 1896. He is best known for writing *The Great Gatsby*, a story about the disillusionment of the American dream. He also wrote *This Side of Paradise, Tender is the Night*, and *The Last Tycoon*.

Fleming, Sir Alexander: Physician. Born in Scotland in 1881. He attended St. Amry's Medical

School, London University. During World War I he served in the Army Medical Corps. His most important contribution to medicine was his discovery of penicillin, which he discovered from studying mold that had grown accidentally on a plate. He was knighted in 1944, and in 1945 he shared the Nobel Prize in Medicine with two others for his work with penicillin.

Ford, Madox: Contemporary novelist, poet, literary critic, and editor. One of the founding fathers of English Modernism. He published over 80 books.

Franklin, Benjamin: Born in Boston in 1706. He published the famous *Poor Richard's Almanac* from 1732 to 1757. In addition to being a publisher, he was also an accomplished scientist. During the Revolutionary War, he was a delegate to the Second Continental Congress, and served on the committee that drafted the Declaration of Independence. After the war, he participated in the Constitutional Convention, and was the only man to serve on both the Second Continental Congress and the Constitutional Convention.

Fripp, Robert: Contemporary guitarist. He is best known as a founder and continuing member of King Crimson.

Fuller, Margaret: Writer. Born in Massachusetts in 1810. She was the editor of Emerson's *The Dial* from 1840 to 1842, and she was also the first literary critic for the *New York Tribune*. In 1845 she wrote *Women in the 19th Century*, which reflected her strong feminist beliefs.

Gaja, Angelo: Contemporary Italian winemaker.

Galileo: Scientist. Born in Pisa in 1564. He was a professor of mathematics at the University of Pisa from 1589 to 1592, and the chair of mathematics at the University of Padua from 1592 to 1610. He built his own telescope, with which he discovered mountains and craters on the moon, saw that the Milky Way was composed of stars, studied spots on the sun, and discovered the four largest satellites of Jupiter. He published his findings in *The Starry Messenger* in 1610. It was his belief in the Copernican notion that the Earth revolved around the Sun that got him into trouble with the Catholic Church. He was warned in 1616 not to advocate this position, which the Church considered heretical. In 1632 he was called before the Inquisition. He was forced, under the threat of torture to abjure his theory. He was sentenced to life imprisonment, and died under house arrest in 1642.

Gay, John (1685-1732): English poet and dramatist. With Swift and Pope Gay formed the group of Tory satirists called the Scriblerians. He is best known for his *Beggar's Opera*, a parody of the newly fashionable Italian opera, which portrays London's criminal lowlife.

Goddard, Lord: English Barrister who became a judge.

Goethe, Johann Wolfgang Von: Poet and writer. Born in Frankfurt in 1749. In addition to studying law, he wrote many poems and stories, and became one of the most famous German writers. He served as chief minister of state in Weimar for 10 years. He is best known for his poem *Faust*.

Greene, Albert Gorton: Writer. Born in 1802. He graduated from Brown University in 1820. After passing the bar exam in 1823, he began to practice law. He served as Clerk of the City Council of Providence, and also as Clerk of the Municipal Court. He edited *The Literary Journal* and *Weekly Register of Science and Arts*, and wrote the poem *Old Grimes is Dead*.

Greene, Gael: Contemporary writer. She was a *New York Magazine's* restaurant critic for more than 30 years. Her weekly column in *New York Magazine* was called "The Insatiable Critic."

Gronow, Captain R.H.: Born in 1794. His memoirs, written in the 1860s, were written in four volumes and detailed his life from 1810 to 1860 during the Regency and Victorian period.

Hamill, Peter: Writer. Wrote the book *Snow in August.*

Harrington, Sir John (1561-1612): English Elizabethan courtier, translator, author, and invented the flush toilet.

Harris, Frank: Writer. Born in Galway, Ireland in 1856. He had a reputation as a womanizer. He wrote a biography on Oscar Wilde that is still popular today. He also wrote a series of biographies on men such as George Bernard Shaw, H.G. Wells, Winston Churchill, and Walt Whitman. His autobiography, *My Life and Loves*, was banned from England and the United States for many years due to its erotic nature.

Harris, Phil: Musician. Born in Linton, Indiana in 1904, and spent much of his childhood in Nashville. His long career in show business began as a bandleader. From 1936 to 1952, he was a regular on the *Jack Benny* radio program as a comedian known for his one liners. He had several hit records, including "The Thing" and "Smoke! Smoke! Smoke that Cigarette". In 1967 he provided the voice of Baloo the Bear in Disney's movie *The Jungle Book*.

Haydn, Joseph: Musician and composer. Born in Austria in 1732. He became a choirboy for the Viennese Cathedral at the age of eight. He was a close friend and mentor of Mozart.

Healy, Maurice: Author. Wrote the 1940 book *Stay Me With Flagons*.

Hemingway, Ernest: Pulitzer and Nobel Prize-winning author. He is considered one of the pre-eminent writers of the 20th century, though his exploits off the written page have drawn equal attention. Born in Oak Park, Illinois in 1899. With the outbreak of World War I, he embarked on a chapter of his life marked by war and turmoil that remained constant throughout his life. *A Farewell to Arms* and *For Whom the Bell Tolls* chronicle World War I and the Spanish Civil War, respectively. His bold lifestyle, which often circled around some type of death, captured the popular attention and added fuel to his celebrity. His life ended as it was lived, violently, with his suicide by shotgun on July 2, 1961.

Henly, William Ernest: English poet and editor. Born in 1849. His poems include "England, My England" and "Invictus."

Heraclitus: Greek philosopher who lived from 535 to 475 B.C.

Herford, Oliver: Contemporary writer. He is responsible for such quotes as "only the young die good," and "a hair in the head is worth two in the brush."

Herodotus: Historian. Born in Greece around 484 B.C. Became known for his travels to such regions as Mesopotamia, Babylon, Athens, Egypt and the Black Sea. In 443 he helped found the colony of Thurii in Italy. He is called the Father of History, as he wrote the first narrative history. His writings focused on the Persian War, but also detailed the growth and history of Greece, Persia, Egypt, Babylon, and Thrace, as well as the pyramids.

Herrick, Robert (1591-1674): Cleric and poet. Born in London in 1591. He wrote on a number of themes like the attributes of young women, rural life, and religious themes and in his later life on his approaching death. He is best known for his poem, "Carpe Diem", made famous in the movie "Dead Poets Society".

Hippocrates: Born around 460 B.C. in Greece. He practiced medicine, and was a strong believer in studying scientific causes for medical problems, rather than attributing them to the gods. The Hippocratic Oath which doctors take today bears his name.

Hoffman, Charles Fenno (1806-1884): Writer. Born in New York. In 1833, he established the well-known *Knickerbocker Magazine* and later edited the *American Monthly Magazine*. In his poetic works, Hoffman's genre of choice was the song. Many of his popular poems were collected in *The Vigil of Faith and Other Poems* (1842).

Holmes, Jack D. L.: Contemporary writer. Wrote numerous articles on the Spanish influence in early colonial America, including a study of the Spanish regulation of the liquor trade.

Homer: Poet in ancient Greece. It is believed he wrote the *Iliad* and the *Odyssey*.

Horace (65-8 B.C.): Latin poet. Among his books of poetry were the first and second books of *Satires*, the four books of *Odes*, and the *Ars Poetica*.

Howell, James: 17th Century writer. He wrote *Epistolae Ho-Eianae. Familiar Letters, Domestic and Forren* while in prison in the 1640s. This book discusses the reign of English Kings James I and Charles I, as well as various other political and philosophical subjects.

Hugo, Victor: Writer. Born in Besacon, France in 1802. At the age of 15 he was honored by the French Academy for a poem he had written. He was elected to the Constitutional Assembly and Legislative Assembly of France's Second Republic. He fled Paris and lived in exile for over 15 years after Napoleon III took power. He returned to France after Napoleon III fell from power, and was elected to the Senate. He is perhaps best known for writing *The Hunchback of Notre Dame* and *Les Miserables*.

Huxley, Aldous: Born in England in 1894. He wanted to study medicine, but was prevented from doing so by a severe eye ailment that nearly blinded him. So, he turned to writing instead. His writing reflected his disillusionment with modern society. He is probably best known for writing *Brave New World*.

James, Walter: Australian contemporary writer. His vast knowledge of wine was reflected in his books. In 1967, *The Walter James Wynn Winegrowers Diary*, which details innovations in the wine industry, was first published. His other writings include: *Barrel and Book*, *A Winemaking Diary*, *Nuts on Wine*, *Wine in Australia*, *What's What About Wine*.

Jefferson, Thomas: Politician. Born in 1743 in Virginia. Graduated from William and Mary. He served in the Second Continental Congress during the Revolutionary War, where he wrote the Declaration of Independence. He served as Secretary of State from 1790-1793; Vice-President from 1796-1800; and was the third President of the United States from 1801-1809. Among his many notable achievements was the founding of the University of Virginia.

Saint Jerome: Religious writer. Born around 347. In 375 he had a vision of Christ. He renounced his pagan studies and fled to the desert to study the scripture. After returning from the desert, he served as a papal secretary to Pope Damasus I, who had him write a new version of the Bible.

Johnson, Hugh: Contemporary writer. He began acquiring his knowledge of wine as a member of the Wine and Food Society at Cambridge University. In 1963, he succeeded

André Simon as editor of *Wine and Food*. With the publication of his first book, *Wine*, (1966), he established himself, at the age of 27, as one of the subject's foremost writers. He has won various awards including the André Simon Prize 1967/1989, The Wines and Vines Trophy 1982, Decanter Magazine Man of the Year 1995, and The International Wine and Spirit Competition 1998 Communicator of the Year.

Johnson, Robert Underwood: American poet. Born in 1853. He served as ambassador to Italy from 1920 to 1921. Among the many poems he wrote are "The Housatonic At Stockbridge," "St. Gaudens, An Ode," and "Luck and Work."

Johnson, Samuel: 18th Century English poet, essayist, critic, journalist, and lexicographer. His appetite was legendary, and it is said that he often drank over 25 cups of tea at one sitting. In 1755 he wrote *The Dictionary of the English Language*, which is often called the first English dictionary. He also wrote *The Lives of The Poets*, a series of biographies of English poets including Dryden, Pope, Swift, and Gay.

Joyce, James: Writer. Born in Dublin in 1882. He was educated at Jesuit schools, including University College, Dublin. Raised in the Roman Catholic faith, he broke with the church while he was in college. In 1904, he left Dublin with Nora Barnacle, a chambermaid whom he eventually married. His first book, the poems of *Chamber Music*, was published in London in 1907, and *Dubliners*, a book of stories in 1914. He is best known for his epic work *Ulysses*.

Kaufman, William I.: Contemporary writer. He is responsible for writing books about food and wine such as *Encyclopedia of American Wine, California Wine Drinks*, and *Gourmet Fondue Cookbook*.

Kazantzakis, Nikos: Greek novelist, poet, and thinker. Born in Crete in 1883. His writings include *Zorba the Greek, The Last Temptation of Christ, Freedom and Death, The Greek Passion*, and his autobiography *Report to Greco*.

Keats, John: Poet. Born in London in 1795. He studied to be a surgeon and became a licensed druggist, but he decided instead on a career as a poet. Among his works are "Lamia", "The Eve of St. Agnes", and "Hyperion".

Keynes, John Maynard: Economist. Born in Cambridge, England in 1883. He is thought of as one of the most influential economists of the 20th century. He was an advisor to the treasury during World War I, and he was part of the Versailles

Peace Conference. He wrote *The Economic Consequences of the Peace*.

Khan, Aga III: Politician. Born in Karachi, India in 1877. In 1885 he became imam of the Nizari Isma'ilite sect at the age of eight. He became known as a leading voice of the Muslim Minority in India, and he served as president of the All-India Muslim league. He was given the title of Sir by the British. In 1937 he represented the British Indian government in the ill-fated League of Nations.

King, Ross: Contemporary entrepreneur. He began his career in the entertainment industry early, as he did his first stage performance at the age of 5 and his first radio broadcast at the age of 15. He has presented numerous radio shows in Britain. He has also presented a wide variety of television shows.

King, Stephen: Writer. Born in Portland, Maine in 1947. His horror stories have made him one of the most popular writers of today. He has lived in Maine most of his life.

Kramer, Matt: Contemporary writer. He has written several books about wine, including: *Making Sense of Wine*, *Making Sense of Burgundy*, and *Making Sense of California Wine*.

Lagasse, Emeril: Contemporary chef. He is credited with revitalizing Creole-Acadian cooking. Now chef/proprietor of three New Orleans and two Las Vegas restaurants, he opened his flagship restaurant, Emeril's, in the New Orleans warehouse district in 1990. Host of the Food Network's highest-rated programs, *The Essence of Emeril* and *Emeril Live*, he won the 1997 Cable Ace Award for "Best Informational Series."

La Guardia, Fiorello: Politician. Born in New York City in 1882. Became active in politics and served in the U.S. House of Representatives from 1917-21 and 1923-33. In 1933, he was elected on a ticket to replace the corrupt Jimmy Walker as mayor of New York. He cleaned up New York government and was renowned for his hard work and great energy. He remains enshrined in the hearts of New Yorkers as one of the city's most popular mayors.

Lamb, Douglas: Writer. Wrote the book *A Pub on Every Corner.*

Launay, Andre: British writer who wrote under such names as Droo Launay and Drew Lanmark. Among his novels are *The Snake Orchids*, *The Medusa Horror*, and *I Married a Model*, a collection of cartoons.

Lehmusvuori, Hannu: Contemporary wine expert who has his own web site where he picks his "Wine of the Week."

Le Gallienne, Richard: Poet and author. Born in England in 1866, and later moved to the United States. His works include *The Romantic Nineties, Quest of a Golden Girl,* and *Volumes in Folio.*

Lewis, Joe E.: Contemporary comedian who was responsible for such quotes as "There is only one thing money won't buy, and that is poverty." Frank Sinatra portrayed him in the movie *The Joker is Wild.*

Lichine, Alexis: French author who wrote several books on wine in the mid-to-late twentieth century. His works include *Alexis Lichine's Encyclopedia of Wines and Spirits* and *Alexis Lichine's Guide to the Wines and Vineyards of France.*

Lichtenberg, G.C. (1742-1799): German physicist and philosopher.

Liebig, Justus: German chemist from the 19th century who developed ground-breaking theories in the field of organic chemistry.

Liebling, A.J. (1904-1963): A war correspondent, a boxing expert, a world-class eater, and for many years at *The New Yorker*, a critic of the press.

Livingstone, Belle: Famous for singing in nightclubs in the 1920s.

Loftus, Simon: A friend of, and the writer of the obituary for Jini Fiennes. Author of *Anatomy of the Wine Trade*.

London, Jack: Writer. Born in San Francisco in 1876. He went to Japan as a seamen at the age of 17. He was a newspaper correspondent during the Russo-Japanese War, and in 1914 he was a war correspondent in Mexico. An avid outdoorsman and adventurer, he became one of America's most famous authors, writing such stories such as *The Call of the Wild*, *Sea Wolf*, and *White Fang*. He struggled with alcoholism later in life, and committed suicide in 1920.

Longfellow, Henry Wadsworth (1807-1882): Writer. Born in Portland, Maine. In 1825, he graduated from Bowdoin College, where he had been classmates with Nathaniel Hawthorne.

Lucia, Salvatore P.: Wrote the book, *Wine & Your Well-Being*.

 **Luther, Martin**: Born on November 10, 1483. He was a German priest and scholar who doubted the practices of the Catholic church. He spread his ideas out to the people. Eventually, these ideas led to the Protestant Revolution. He gained fame as one who wanted to bring back the foundations on which the Roman Catholic Church had been established but which (according to him) it had lost during its long life. He succeeded and even today various branches of Protestantism are spread throughout the world.

Maccius, Titus: Writer. Born in Sarsina as Plautus. He joined the Roman soldiers, where he was exposed to the Greek theater. At 45, he was able to become a full-time playwright. He wrote plays that involved a continuously evolving plot, cheap slapstick, and anything else that would keep the audience at attention and laughing. Each of his plays had a musical accompaniment, but none of the musical pieces survived to this day. Later on, Plautus was granted Roman citizenship and allowed to take three names, as a true Roman. He named himself "Titus Maccius" (to which he added his existing name) which, when translated, literally means "clown."

Mackay, Charles (1814–1889): Scottish poet, journalist, and editor. Best known for his verses. His book, *Memoirs of Extraordinary Popular Delusions*, was first published in 1841.

Malvezin, Theophile: He is quoted as saying "Wine is made to be drunk as women are made to be loved; profit by the freshness of youth and of the splendor of maturity; do not await decrepitude."

Marx, Karl (1818-1883): Philosopher, social scientist, historian and revolutionary. He is without a doubt the most influential socialist thinker to emerge in the 19th century. Although he was largely ignored by scholars in his own lifetime, his social, economic and political ideas gained rapid acceptance in the socialist movement after his death in 1883. With Engels as his closest collaborator and disciple, he reorganized the Communist League, which met in London in 1847. In 1848, he finalized the *Communist Manifesto*, which attacked the state as the instrument of oppression, and religion and culture as ideologies of the capitalist class. He was expelled from Brussels, and in 1849 settled in London, where he studied economics, and wrote the first volume of his major work, *Das Kapital*.

Mather, Increase: Writer. Born in 1693. He had serious doubts as to whether or not the Salem Witch Trials actually served justice. In 1764, he published an essay that shifted the blame for the Indian Wars and droughts not on the accused witches, but on the people themselves, and on their committed sins, for which these disasters were punishment.

Matthews, Thomas: Contemporary editor. He is the senior editor of *"The Wine Spectator."* He has published several reports on the finest restaurants in France, America and England.

Maximovich, Milan: Winemaker, acclaimed for his Thunder Mountain 1998 Merlot.

McCarthy, M.J.F.: Contemporary writer and chef. He is the owner of the high-class restaurant "Michael's" in Santa Barbara, California. He graduated from the Ecole Hotelier de Paris, the Cordon Bleu, and the Academie du Vin. He is the author of a cookbook, *Michael's Cookbook: The Art of New American Food and Contemporary Entertaining from the Creator of Michael's Restaurant.*

McDougall, James A.: Born in New York in 1817. He studied law and became Attorney General of Illinois in 1842. He then moved to California and became head of the California bar. He later served in Congress, first in the House of Representatives, and then as a Senator from the state of California.

McNulty, Henry: Contemporary writer. Author of *Vogue Cocktails*. He lives in Philadelphia, Pennsylvania, and besides writing books on wine, broadcasts a radio show on food and wines.

Meisel, Anthony: Author of *American Wine*.

Meyer, Justin: Winemaker. He is a former member of the Christian Brothers religious order, which he joined in his quest for the finest wine-making skills. After spending 15 years with the order, he left it and purchased a winery. Instead of making several different wines, he committed himself to one – Cabernet – and has made this fact one of his primary advertisements.

Michelangelo (1475-1564): Born in 1475, in Caprese in the rural Tuscany region of Italy. He was the greatest sculptor of the 16th century, and also one of the greatest painters, architects, and poets, making him one of the greatest artists to ever live.

Millay, Edna St. Vincent: Contemporary writer. Graduated from Vassar. She wrote several collections of poetry, each of which had a strong feminist inclination and were very well-received.

Milton, John: Writer. Born in London in 1608 and attended St. Paul's School and Christ's College, Cambridge. In 1638 he traveled to Italy, where he met Galileo. He supported the Presbyterians efforts to reform the Church of England. He held a position in Oliver Cromwell's government as Latin Secretary of Foreign Affairs. He spent many years writing his two greatest works, *Paradise Lost* and *Paradise Regained*.

Mizner, Wilson (1876-1933): American dramatist and con-artist, he was born in Benecia, California. He became a co-owner of the Brown Derby restaurant, but he was better known for his unscrupulous schemes, like rigging fights so he could win the bets, running a gambling establishment in Long Island, and selling fake Spanish architecture to a number of wealthy people. He is best known today for his quotes, such as "when you steal from one author, it's plagiarism; when you steal from many, it's research."

Moliere: Writer. Born in Paris in 1622. His real name was Jean Baptiste Poquelin. He studied law, but decided instead on a career in the theatre. He became known, however, for producing and participating in great comedic plays, among them *Le Misanthrope* and *Le Docteur Amoreux*.

Mondavi, R. Michael: Winemaker. Born in 1912. His parents were Italian and had moved to Minnesota from Italy in 1910. In 1946, he and his father purchased the Charles Krug Winery. He was a big fan of innovation, and was the first to popularize both the cold fermentation method and the Chenin Blanc wine. He was also the first American winemaker to start using small barrels for aging wines instead of 5,000 gallon tankers as had been done previously. He has been a strong advocate of the moderate consumption of wine, and the enjoyment of wine with food.

Mondavi, Robert G.: Winemaker. Stalwart of the California wine industry. Responsible in substantial part for fashioning the high quality and polished style of today's California wines. He and his family initiated or popularized dozens of now widely accepted wine making practices (like cold fermentation of white wines, non-filtration of reds, and close planting of grape vines) that brought California wines into the modern era in the 1960s and 1970s.

Mondavi, Timothy: Son of Robert Mondavi. He is Vice-Chairman and Winegrower of the Robert Mondavi Corporation. Having graduated from the University of California, he joined the company in 1974, and four years later became a member of the Board of Directors. He has remained in that position to this day.

Montague, Charles Edward: Writer. Born in 1867. In 1890, he joined the Manchester Guardian, and soon thereafter became assistant editor. With him as one of its officials, the Guardian became a political campaigning newspaper. Aside from politics, he wrote about theater, and by the early 1900's was known as Great Britain's leading critic of drama.

Moore, Thomas (1779-1852): Poet, lyricist, composer, and satirist. Born in Dublin, Ireland. His major works included *Irish Melodies* and *Cash, Corn, and Catholics*. He devoted much of his work to support Irish nationalism.

Morgan, Sydney Owenson (1776-1859): Writer. She first emerged into the world as a writer with her 1806 novel *The Wild Irish Girl*. In addition to her novels, she wrote several volumes of poetry and memoirs.

Mortimer, John (1740-1779): Painter. He was a student of Reynolds and a painter of portraits, as well as religious subjects.

Mortimer, John: Born in 1923, he was an English barrister. He wrote plays for the theater, for television, as well as for movies and radio. Apart from these plays, he has branched out more than once to write a novel or an autobiographical work.

Neal, John Mason: Writer. Born in London in 1818. He studied at Cambridge and became warden of Sacville College in East Grinstead. He wrote several books on church history, as well as a great number of hymns. One of his most well-known hymns is "Jerusalem the Golden."

Niven, David: Actor. Born in 1909, in Kirriemuir, Angus, Scotland, he died on July 29, 1983, in Château-d'Oex, Switzerland. Born to a family of military service, he attended the Sandhurst Military Academy. Still, he did not follow in his family's footsteps and instead, sometime in the 1930s, made his way to Hollywood. He had a steady stream of jobs coming to him and became well-known as a light comedy actor.

O'Malley, Austin: Born in 1760, United Irish leader.

O'Malley, Austin: Born in 1859. Served as a professor of English studies at Notre Dame.

Ombiaux, Maurice des (1898-1943): Writer. He was attracted by the literary revival of the

1880's. His works include poetry, prose, the retellings of legend, and other styles.

Orwell, George (1903-1950): English Novelist, essayist, and critic famous for his political satire: *Animal Farm* and *1984*. He was educated in England at Eton College. After his education, he served in the Indian Imperial Police from 1922-1927. Upon return to England, he lived in poverty before finding work as a teacher at a private school.

Osler, William: Canadian physician. He graduated from McGill University in 1872. He was a professor at McGill (1875-84), the University of Pennsylvania (1884-89), Johns Hopkins (1889-1904), and Oxford (from 1905). He was knighted in 1911. In 1892 he wrote the medical textbook *The Principles and Practice of Medicine*, which became a very influential book.

Ovid: Ancient Roman poet. Born in 43 B.C. He lived in Rome until the age of 50, when he was banished to Tomi. He is best known for writing *Metamorphosis*, a series of poems about Greek and Roman legends.

Parker, Dorothy: Author. Born (Dorothy Rothschild) in 1893. Her brother died on the Titanic in 1912. In 1915, her poem was published in *Vanity Fair*. She wrote her first short story, "Such a

Pretty Little Thing," in 1919. In 1922, she became the only female founding member of the Algonquin Round Table, a coalition of authors. She went on to write several books of poetry and some of prose.

Parker, Robert: Born in 1947. He studied law at the University of Maryland Law School and was Senior Attorney as well as Assistant General Counsel for the Farm Credit Banks of Baltimore. In 1985, he published the world-acclaimed book *Bordeaux*. He went on to write several more renowned wine books, as well as four editions of his wine guides. In 1999, he was awarded the *Legion D'Honneur* (Honor Legion), France's highest award.

Pascal: Scientist. Born in 1623, in Clermont-Ferrand, France, he died on August 19, 1662, in Paris. He was a mathematician, a physician, and a writer. His theories led the way to modern theories of probabilities. He also discovered what is today known as Pascal's Law of Pressure. His inventions included the syringe, a calculating machine, and the barometer.

Pasteur, Louis: French chemist. Born in 1822. After being asked by Napoleon III to study the diseases that were damaging France's wine industry, he discovered that the damage was done by microorganisms that could be killed by heating the wine to 55 degrees Celsius. This process became known as Pasteurization. Among his many other achievements was the development of vaccines for rabies, anthrax and chicken cholera. In 1887 the Pasteur Institute was founded as a teaching and research center for infectious diseases.

Pater, Walter: English writer and critic. Born in London in 1839. He attended Queen's College, Oxford in 1858. He wrote such books as *The Renaissance*, *Marius the Epicurean*, and *Appreciations*.

Peacock, Thomas Love (1785-1866): Satirist, essayist, and poet. He wrote both prose and poetry. Self-taught, he was one of the most scholarly and philosophical of 19th century writers.

Pelligrini, Angelo: Contemporary writer. He is the author of the book *Lean Years Happy Years*, which advocates a principle of growing, cooking, and making one's own wine.

Pepys, Samuel: Writer. Born in 1633, in London, England. What little is known about him today is taken from his diaries, which are now housed in his former college.

Pérignon, Dom Pierre (1638-1714): Benedictine monk in the 17th century. He and his brethren discovered that the phenomenon of sparkling wines bursting open their containers was occurring due to carbon dioxide pressure buildup. He recommended the successful method of using cork stoppers tied down with string. He was one of the pioneers of blending the wines of Champagne.

Pépin, Jacques: Contemporary host of award-winning cooking shows on national public television, master chef, food columnist, cooking teacher, and author of nineteen cookbooks. Born in Bourg-en-Bresse, near Lyon. At age 13, he began his formal apprenticeship at the distinguished Grand Hotel de L'Europe in his hometown. He subsequently worked in Paris, training under Lucien Diat at the Plaza Athénée. From 1956 to 1958, he was the personal chef to three French heads of state, including Charles de Gaulle. He moved to the United States in 1959, and served for ten years as director of research and new development for the Howard Johnson Company. He and Julia Child co-hosted a twenty-two show PBS-TV series entitled *Julia and Jacques Cooking at Home*.

Perez, Antonio (1534-1611): Born in Madrid, Spain. He was the Spanish courtier to Phillip II. He was the illegitimate son of Gonzalo Perez, secretary to Phillip's predecessor. After rising quickly in Phillip's service, he became a fugitive from the court and fled to France.

Petronius: Roman writer. Born in 27 A.D. He served as an advisor to the emperor Nero. He had a reputation of enjoying a life of luxury and partying. He is best known for writing the *Satrycon*, a satire of life in the Roman Empire.

Peynaud, Emile: Contemporary French enologist who wrote the book, *The Taste of Wine*, and has been quoted in many wine-tasting manuals.

Plat, Sir Hugh: Writer. He was an enthusiastic gardener, and his gardens at Bishop's Hall were celebrated. His books, *The Jewel House of Art and Nature*, *Floraes Paradise*, *Garden of Eden*, exhibit his dedication and love of gardens. His herb gardens were his chief love and were extolled in his book, *Delights for Ladies*, which consisted entirely of herb recipes.

Plato: Greek philosopher. He lived from around 427 B.C. to 347 B.C. His mentor was Socrates. He is widely considered one of the greatest philosophers of all time, and his writings are still influential on modern philosophers. He founded a school called The Academy, where he taught philosophy and mathematics.

Pliny the Elder: Roman writer. Born in 23 A.D., he served in the Roman army as a cavalry commander. After leaving the army, he returned to

Rome to study law. He is best known for writing *The Natural History*. This collection of 37 books discusses such topics as geography, zoology, anthropology, and the nature of the physical universe. He died in 79 A.D. in the eruption of Mt. Vesuvius in Pompei.

Po, Li Tai: Chinese poet from the 8th century. While his works include many traditional forms of poetry, he is best known for his imaginative pieces filled with compelling emotions and expressive Taoist images.

Pollman, Mark: Author of *Bottled Wisdom*, a collection of anecdotes, humor and advice about drinking.

Pompadour, Madame de: Courtesan. Born in France in 1721. In 1745 she became the mistress of King Louis XV, and exerted some influence over state policy, such as encouraging France's alliance with Austria.

Pope, Alexander: Poet. Born in London, England in 1688. A tubercular disease stunted his growth at four feet six inches. He became one of the best known poets of his day, and his writings include *Pastorals*, *An Essay on Criticism*, and *The Dunciad*. He later re-translated Homer's *The Iliad* and *The Odyssey*.

Pope John XXIII: Angelo Giuseppe Roncalli was born in Italy in 1881. He served as Pope from 1958 until his death in 1963. The high point of his reign was the convening of the ecumenical council in 1962.

Pope Pius XII: Eugenio Pacelli was born in Rome in 1876, and was ordained in 1899. From 1904 to 1916, he helped Cardinal Gasperri to codify cannon law. In 1929 he became a cardinal in the church. In 1930, he became the Secretary of State for Vatican City, and became Pope Pius XII in 1939.

Prial, Frank J.: Writer. Writes a column on wine for the *New York Times*.

Rabelais, Francois (1494-1553): French writer and satirist. He spent time in a Franciscan monastery, where his studies included law, science, Greek and Latin. He received his bachelor of medicine in 1530. In 1532 he wrote *Pantagruel*, a story about a young giant.

Rainbird, George: Writer. He wrote *An Illustrated Guide to Wine*, and *The Subtle Alchemist: A Book of Wine*.

Ray, Cyril: Writer. He wrote quite a few books on various alcoholic drinks, including, *Robert Mondavi of the Napa Valley, Bolliner, Tradition of a Champagne Family, Cognac, Complete Book of Spirits and Liquors, Cyril Ray's Boor of Wine*, and others.

Redding, Cyrus: 19th century journalist, wine connoisseur, and author. *A History & Description of Modern Wine*, written by Redding, is a fabulous early 19th treatise on important wines of time.

Rice, Elmer: American dramatist who incorporated his law degree into a career in the world of theater. He served as the regional director of the New York Federal Theater Project in the 1930's.

Cardinal Richelieu: Cardinal of the Roman Catholic Church in 1622 and two years later secured the position of Chief Minister to France's King Louis XIII. Despite opposition from the King's mother, Marie de' Medici, Richelieu eventually gained complete governmental control. Although he strengthened France's naval and armed forces, people were dissatisfied with this rule because he brought the country into the Thirty Years' War and depleted the nation's finances.

Robinson, Janice: Wine writer and broadcaster with an international reputation. She was *Decanter* magazine's 1999 Woman of the Year. She was also voted first ever Television Personality of the Year in the 1999 Glenfiddich Awards for food and drink media. She has been a columnist for both *The Sunday Times* of London and the American *Wine Spectator* and now writes for *The Financial Times* as well as a column that is published by 12 magazines in five continents.

Rogers, Will (1879-1935): American entertainer. Famous for his pithy and homespun humor, he became famous in the sound films: *A Connecticut Yankee* and *State Fair*. He was also a star of Broadway and 71 movies of the 1920s and 1930s.

Rosenzweig, Sheila: Writer of the book *American Wine*, which is considered to be one of the best books covering domestic wines.

Rothschild, Philippe de: Founder of the famous wine company that still bears his name today.

Rudofsky, Bernard: Author of the books *The Kimono Mind, Now I Lay Me Down to Eat, Architecture Without Architects*, and others.

St. John, Bill: Lives in Denver, Colorado and is a restaurant reviewer for a local television station there. He writes a column for *Wine and Spirits*

Magazine called "Fearless Omnivore." He is also the author of a collection of dining reviews called *Bill St. John's Rocky Mountain Restaurants*.

Saintsbury, George: Born in Southampton, England in 1845. He began his career as a teacher, and became a well-known critic of French and English literature. He served as a professor of rhetoric and English literature from 1895 to 1915.

Sassoon, Siegfried (1886-1967): English writer and poet. He was an officer in the British Army during World War I. His experiences in the war led him to write about the horrors he had witnessed in *The Old Huntsman, Counter-Attack, Satirical Poems*, and *Vigils*.

Schoonmaker, Frank: Author of *The New Frank Schoonmaker Encyclopedia of Wine, Encyclopedia of Wine*, and *Frank Schoonmaker's Encyclopedia of Wine*. He was considered to be one of the greatest wine authorities and winemakers of his time and his first wine encyclopedia was published in 1964.

Scott, Sir Walter (1771-1832): Writer. Born in Edinburgh, Scotland. He studied law at Edinburgh University from 1783. He continued in his legal career until retiring in 1830. He created and popularized historical novels in a series called the *Waverley Novels*.

Shakespeare, William: Writer, poet. Born in Stratford-upon-Avon, Warwickshir, England in 1564. He moved to London and became part of the theater company Lord Chamberlin's Men (which later became the King's Men) as an actor and playwright. The popularity of his plays allowed him and six others to buy The Globe, an outdoor theater. He is considered by many to be one of the greatest writers of all time.

Shaw, George Bernard: Writer. Born in Dublin, Ireland in 1856. He became a famous playwright, known for stories that satirized English society. A committed socialist, he was criticized for his opposition to World War I. His most famous plays include *The Devil's Disciple*, *Man and Superman*, *Major Barbara*, and *Pygmalion*.

Shaw, T.G.: In 1863, he wrote *Wine, Vine and the Cellar*.

Sheridan, Richard Brinsley: English dramatist and politician. He spent a few years writing and directing for the Drury Lane Theater. His works include *The Rivals* and *The School for Scandal*. In 1780, he entered Parliament, thereby broadening his career to include a life of politics.

Shor, Toots (1904-1977): Owner of a New York bar that was the favorite of many of the area's professional and other baseball players. After a while, he became one of the most often-quoted observers of the games.

Sichel, Allan: Contemporary writer. He first wrote and published the "Vintage Report," a yearly report that uses the crop, the weather, the wine, and the market to draw conclusions on the price of the wine and its quality. This "Vintage Report" is published to this day.

Sichel, Peter: Bordeaux wine merchant whose family owned a part interest in Château Palmer, and who owned Château d'Angludet. He was an exponent of Bordeaux and served as president of the influential Union des Grands Crus.

Simon, André (1877-1970): Gourmet, wine connoisseur, historian and writer. He is unrivaled in his contribution to the "art of good living." Born in Paris, he came to London in 1902 as the English agent for the champagne house of Pommery and Greno. He wrote over 100 books and pamphlets on wine and food.

Saint Simon: One of the 12 disciples in the New Testament.

Sina, Ibn of Afshena: Born in 980, he is also known as Avicenna. He was an Arab philosopher and physician whose name carried much influence in the fields of philosophy and medicine. His masterpieces include *Canon of Medicine* and *Book of Healing*.

Smith, Adam: Born in 1723, he was an Oxford-educated economist and philosopher. He gained international acclaim through his ideas in *Theory of Moral Sentiments*. He is best known for the laissez-faire economic theories he expressed in *The Wealth of Nations*.

Socrates: Greek philosopher from the 5th century B.C. who believed so strongly in his ideas that he ultimately gave up his life in their defense. He viewed philosophy as a necessary factor in the lives of all intelligent men.

Sokolin, William: The nation's leading fine wine merchant and investor.

Starr, Kevin: Currently is a Professor at the University of Southern California in Los Angeles, and a contributing editor to the Opinion section of the *Los Angeles Times*. Author of *Americans and the California Dream, 1850 – 1915*, his writings have won him a Guggenheim Fellowship, membership in the Society of American Historians, and the Gold Medal of the Commonwealth Club in California. He is a long-time state librarian of California.

Steadman, Ralph: Writer. Born in 1936.
He started as a cartoonist and through the years
expanded into many fields of creativity. He has
illustrated such classics as *Alice in Wonderland, Treasure
Island,* and *Animal Farm.* His own books include the
lives of Sigmund Freud, Leonardo da Vinci and *The
Big I Am,* the story of God. Also, he is a printmaker.
His prints include a series of etchings on writers
from William Shakespeare to William Burroughs.
He has traveled the world's vineyards and
distilleries for Oddbins, which culminated in his
two prize-winning books, *The Grapes of Ralph* and
Still Life With Bottle.

Sterling, George (1869-1926): A poet, born
in Long Island, New York. He became friends with
the writer Jack London, who referred to him as
"Greek." In 1903 he wrote *A Wine of Wizardry* which
was not published until 1907. He was a member of
San Francisco's Bohemian Club. Among his many
other writings is the poem "Lilith."

Strauss, Johann I (1804-1849): Musician.
Largely self-taught as a musician, he developed the
waltz in the form and style we associate with the
Strauss family. He wrote 251 opus numbered works
(out of a total of over 300), among them 153
waltzes, the most famous of which is "Lorelei-
Rheinklänge" (Sounds of the Rhine Loreley) (1843).

Stevenson, Robert Louis (1850-1894): Born in 1850 in Scotland. He was best known as the author of *Treasure Island* and *The Strange Case of Dr. Jekyll and Mr. Hyde*, along with *Kidnapped*, and *The Master of Ballantrae*.

Swift, Jonathan: Irish author and satirist. Born in 1667 in Dublin. His first major satirical work, *A Tale of a Tub*, appeared in 1704. In 1710, he became editor of *The Examiner*, the journal of the ruling Tory party. But with the fall of the Tories in 1714, he accepted a post as Dean of St. Patrick's, Dublin. Among his best known works is *Gulliver's Travels*.

Talleyrand: French politician. Best known for his support of the revolutionists in the French revolution. He was the political representative of the clergy, but was excommunicated from the church in 1791. During the political and social turmoil in France at the end of the 18th century, he sought refuge in England and the United States before finally returning to France in 1796.

Tchelistcheff, Andre: Winemaker. Born in Russia. At the age of 17, his family's estate was burned to the ground. He served in the White (anti-communist) army during the Russian Civil War. He was left for dead on the battlefield, and his father even had a funeral for him. But, he survived the war, moved to California, and became a winemaker.

Temple, Sir William: 17th century English politician and author. He joined the Irish parliament and served as a powerful figure in creating alliances among different nations. He stepped out of politics in 1681 and dedicated the remainder of his time to political writing.

Tennyson, Alfred Lord: English poet. Born in 1809. He wrote a poem called "The Devil and the Lady" at the age of 14. In 1827 he attended Cambridge. In 1850 he was appointed poet laureate. His *Idylls the King* detailed the rise and fall of King Arthur. He wrote *Memoriam* about his friend Arthur Hallam's death.

Thackeray, W.M.: English writer. Born in Calcutta, India in 1911. This satirist is known for writing *The Book of Snobs*, *Vanity Fair*, and *The History of Henry Esmond, esq.*

Theognis: Greek philosopher in 6th Century B.C.

Thomas, Dylan: 20th century Welsh poet with a strong voice to match his strong poetry. He both wrote and read for the BBC radio.

Thurber, James (1894-1961): Acknowledged as the greatest American humorist since Mark Twain. His book, *My Life and Hard Times*, helped establish him as a leading humorist and even got him the opportunity to publicize his next book, *Is Sex Necessary* (written with a fellow *New Yorker* writer).

Thurston, E. Temple (1879-1933): Writer. He wrote *The Wandering Jew: A Play in Four Phases*, *The City of Beautiful Nonsense*, *Sally Bishop*, and *Flower of Gloucester*.

Tovey, Charles: English wine merchant. Author of several manuals for wine merchants on the identification of the quality of wines.

Trowbridge, John Townsend (1827-1916): Writer. Born in Arlington, Massachusetts in 1827. His novels include *Neighbor Jackwood*, an antislavery novel; *Lucy Arlyn*; *Coupon Bonds, and Other Stories*; *Farnell's Folly*; and *Neighbors' Wives*. He also was known for his writings on Walt Whitman in *The Atlantic Monthly*.

 **Twain, Mark**: Writer. Born, Samuel Clemens, in 1835. In his boyhood, he trained as a steamboat pilot. He lost and gained fortunes several times, and was always happy to address

students in his many lectures in halls across the United States. He wrote many memorable books and the whole world mourned his death in 1910.

Tyler-Herbst, Sharon: Writer. She, along with her husband, Ron Herbst, authored *Wine Lover's Companion* and *The Ultimate A-Z Bar Guide*. Dubbed the foremost writer of user-friendly food and drink reference works, she is an award-winning author of 13 books.

Tynan, Kenneth: Born in Birmingham, England in 1927. He was a theatre critic, author, and theatrical executive. He wrote for *The London Observer* during the 1950's and became the literary manager of the National Theatre of Great Britain in 1963. During the latter part of his life, he wrote profiles for *The New Yorker*. In addition to these accomplishments, he published several books during his lifetime. One of the most noteworthy was *Curtains*, which was published in 1961.

Venner, Tobias: Writer. Wrote a book, *An Accurate Treatise Concerning Tobacco*, in which he wrote about his conclusion that tobacco had adverse effects on the eyes of people who use it.

Virgil: Roman poet. Born in 70 B.C., in Andes, a village near Mantua in northern Italy. He authored three sets of well-known books: *The*

Eclogues, The Georgics, and *The Aeneid.* His most
famous work, *The Aeneid,* glorifies Rome and
promotes Rome's mission to civilize the world.

Vos, Johann Heinrich (1751-1826): German
poet and philologist. He studied at Göttingen
and in his time as schoolmaster at Otterndorf
(1778) and Eutin (1782), he began a career
translating the classics. In 1805, he became a
professor of classical philology at Heidelberg.
His best-known translations are of the *Odyssey*
(1781) and *The Iliad* (1793).

Waldo, Myra: Writer. She has written several
cooking books, including *Soufflé Cookbook* and
Art of South American Cooking.

Walker, Thomas: Physician, politician. He
graduated from William and Mary, and then studied
medicine. He was the physician of Peter Jefferson,
Thomas Jefferson's father. He became Thomas
Jefferson's guardian after Peter Jefferson's death. He
was well-known as an explorer, and in 1750 he led
an expedition into present day Kentucky. Later in
life he became active in politics, and served in
Virginia's House of Burgess.

Waugh, Auberon: Writer. Born in England
in 1939. Although he lived in the shadow of his

famous father, the novelist Evelyn Waugh, he became a noted writer and critic in his own right. He wrote columns for such magazines as *Spectator*, *Private Eye*, and *The New Statesman*. He founded the magazine *Literary Review*, which annually awarded the novel with the worst sex scene.

Waugh, Evelyn: Born in London, England in 1903. He spent time as a teacher and an art student before finally becoming a writer. His pre-World War II stories were satirical in nature, and include "Decline and Fall", "Black Mischief", and "Scoop". He fought for the British in World War II, and his post war novels took a more serious turn. These novels include *The Brideshead Revisited*, *Men at Arms*, *Officers and Gentlemen*, and *The End of the Battle*.

Webster, John: English dramatist. His life is not well-known but his tragedies are. In particular, he is known for his two greatest works, *The White Devil* and *The Duchess of Malfi*.

Weld, Charles R.: Author who wrote the book *History of the Royal Society*.

Wells, H.G.: Writer. Born in Bromley, Kent. He developed an early taste for literature. He wrote his first book, *The Time Machine*, which gained instant fame and thrust him into the world of literature. Refusing to leave his home during World War II, he wrote his last book, *Mind at the End of its Tether*, after which, in 1946, he died in that same London home.

Wilde, Oscar: Writer. Born in Dublin, Ireland in 1854. He wrote such books as *Poems*, *The Happy Prince*, and *The Picture of Dorian Gray*. He wrote such plays as *Lady Windermere's Fan*, *A Woman of No Importance* and *The Importance of Being Earnest*. He was responsible for such quotes as "Always forgive your enemies. Nothing annoys them more."

Williams, Tennessee: Writer. Born in Columbus, Mississippi in 1911. He graduated from the University of Iowa in 1938, and became one of America's most famous playwrights. The first recognition of his genius came with the 1945 play *The Glass Menagerie*. He won a Pulitzer Prize for his 1947 play *A Streetcar Named Desire*. His later plays include *Cat on a Hot Tin Roof*, *Sweet Bird of Youth*, and *Night of the Iguana*.

Wodehouse, P.G.: Comic novelist. Born in England in 1881. His humorous fiction includes works such as *The Inimitable Jeeves* and *Bertie Wooster Sees It Through*. He moved to the United States when he was in his late 20's and became an American citizen in 1955. His English ties were revived as he was knighted 20 years later.

Woolf, Virginia (1882-1941): British author, distinguished feminist essayist, critic in *The Times Literary Supplement,* and a central figure of Bloomsbury group. Born in London, England. As an essayist, she was prolific authoring and publishing over 500 essays in periodicals. She impacted and innovated 20th century fiction. Her works included *The Voyage Out, Night and Day, Jacob's Room, Mrs. Dalloway, To the Lighthouse, The Waves, Orlando, The Years,* and *Between the Acts.*

Yeats, William Butler: Poet. Born in Dublin, Ireland in 1865. He was interested in Irish culture and history, and became involved in Irish Nationalist Politics. He wrote many of his poems in an attempt to instill his great pride in Ireland in his fellow countrymen. In 1923, he received the Nobel Prize in literature. Collections of his work include *The Wanderings of Oisen, The Celtic Twighlight, In the Seven Woods* and *The Tower.*

Younger, William: Brewer from Edinburgh, Scotland. William Younger & Co. Ltd. still bears his name.

Yutang, Lin: Chinese-American writer, translator, and editor, educated in China and at Harvard. He spent most of his life in the United States and wrote most of his many works in English. His non-fictional books include *My Country*

and My People (1935); *A Leaf in the Storm* (1941), about
war-torn China; *Between Tears and Laughter* (1943), and
The Pleasures of a Nonconformist (1962). Among his
novels are *Chinatown Family* (1948) and *The Flight of
the Innocents* (1965). He translated and edited *The
Chinese Theory of Art* (1968).

Zraly, Kevin: Wine Director of Windows
on the World restaurant, which on September 11,
2001 had the largest wine list in New York City, and
sold more wine than any restaurant in the United
States, since 1976. He wrote the book *Windows on the
World Complete Wine Course*, which has sold over
one million copies. In 1991, he was the Food and
Beverage Association's "Man of the Year" award.